CW00521773

Birth Control & Abortion in Islam

In the name of Allāh,
Most Gracious, Most Merciful.
All praise be to Allāh,
Lord of the Worlds,
and peace and blessings be
upon His Messenger Muḥammad,
Mercy to the Worlds

MUHAMMAD IBN ADAM AL-KAWTHARI

Birth Control & Abortion in Islam

White Thread
PRESS
LONDON

© Muhammad ibn Adam al-Kawthari 2006
First Edition September 2006 Reprint June 2015

All rights reserved. Aside from fair use, meaning a few pages or less for non-profit educational purposes, review, or scholarly citation, no part of this publication may be reproduced, stored in a retrieval system, or transmitted in any form or by any means, electronic, mechanical, photocopying, recording or otherwise, without the prior permission of the copyright owner.

ISBN: 978-1-933764-00-9

Published by:
White Thread Press
White Thread Limited, London, UK
www.whitethreadpress.com
info@whitethreadpress.com

Distributed in the UK by Azhar Academy Ltd. London
www.azharacademy.com Tel: +44 (208) 911 9797

Library of Congress Cataloging-in-Publication Data

Al-Kawthari, Muhammad ibn Adam.
Birth control & abortion in Islam / Muhammad ibn Adam Al-Kawthari. — 1st ed.
p. cm.
Includes index.
ISBN-13: 978-1-933764-00-9 (softcover : alk. paper)
ISBN-10: 1-933764-00-7 (softcover : alk. paper)
1. Birth control (Islamic law) 2. Birth control–Religious aspects–Islam.
3. Abortion (Islamic law) I. Title. II. Title: Birth control and abortion in Islam.
KBP3124.A45 2006
297.5'66–dc22

2006003698

♾ Printed and bound in the United States of America on acid-free paper. The paper used in this book meets the minimum requirement of ANSI/NISO Z39.48-1992 (R 1997) (Permanence of Paper). The binding material has been chosen for strength and durability.

Cover image from iStockphoto
Cover design by CWDM
Book design and typography by ARM

THE MEDICAL INFORMATION in this book is presented to help educate readers on the Islamic laws concerning birth control and abortion and is not a substitute for professional medical advice. The author and White Thread Press are not responsible for any medical decisions or actions taken based on the information in this book.

For my Shaykh

Muftī Shabbir Ahmad,

Ḥadīth teacher at Darul Uloom,

Bury, UK, who was the main

inspiration behind this work

TRANSLITERATION KEY

ء (أ إ) ’ (A slight catch in the breath. It is also used to indicate where the *hamza* has been dropped from the beginning of a word.)

ا a, ā

ب b

ت t

ث th (Should be pronounced as the *th* in *thin* or *thirst.*)

ج j

ح ḥ (Tensely breathed *h* sound.)

خ kh (Pronounced like the *ch* in Scottish *loch* with the mouth hollowed to produce a full sound.)

د d

ذ dh (Should be pronounced as the *th* in *this* or *that.*)

ر r

ز z

س s

ش sh

ص ṣ (A heavy *s* pronounced far back in the mouth with the mouth hollowed to produce a full sound.)

ض ḍ (A heavy *d/dh* pronounced far back in the mouth with the mouth hollowed to produce a full sound.)

ط ṭ (A heavy *t* pronounced far back in the mouth with the mouth hollowed to produce a full sound.)

ظ ẓ (A heavy *dh* pronounced far back in the mouth with the mouth hollowed to produce a full sound.)

ع ʿ, ʿa, ʿi, ʿu (Pronounced from the throat.)

غ gh (Pronounced like a throaty French *r* with the mouth hollowed to produce a full sound.)

ف f

ق q (A guttural *q* sound with the mouth hollowed to produce a full sound.)

ك k

ل l

م m

ن n

و w, ū, u.

ه h

ي y, ī, i

ﷺ *Ṣalla ’Llāhu ʿalayhi wa sallam*—used following the mention of the Messenger Muḥammad, translated as, “May Allāh bless him and give him peace.”

﵇ *ʿAlayhi ’s-sallam*—used following the mention of a Prophet or Messenger of Allāh, translated as, “May the peace of Allāh be upon him.”

ؓ *Raḍiya ’Llāhu ʿanhu*—used following the mention of a Companion of the Messenger, translated as, “May Allāh be pleased with him.”

ؓ *Raḍiya ’Llāhu ʿanhum*—used following the mention of more than one Companion of the Messenger (and also after a female Companion in this work for lack of an appropriate glyph), translated as, “May Allāh be pleased with them.”

Contents

Foreword

In the name of Allāh, Most Compassionate, Most Merciful. All praise is for Allāh Most High, Lord of the worlds, and peace and blessings upon His beloved Messenger Muḥammad, a Mercy to the Worlds ﷺ.

This book is a revised edition of an earlier work that I compiled, titled *Birth Control in Islam*. In 1997, while studying at one of the renowned institutions of Islamic learning in the UK, Darul Uloom in Bury (Lancashire), I was often posed with inquiries concerning contraception and abortion. Several individuals wished to know the Islamic viewpoint on the various forms of contraception and the ruling on abortion. Owing to their interest and the great relevance of the issue to modern-day life, I felt it appropriate to prepare a comprehensive and detailed understanding on these matters. Hence, by the grace of Allāh Almighty, I was able to prepare an article discussing birth control and abortion.

The first impression of this work appeared in a monthly magazine published by the aforementioned institution. Friends and colleagues of mine suggested that I add to it and have it published in the form of a booklet. The suggestion was a laudable one to which I responded positively.

Accordingly, the first edition of this book was published towards the latter part of 1997, and through the grace of Allāh Most High all copies were sold out. However, there were certain deficiencies with the publication.

Firstly, the book was not widely circulated and distributed as it ought to have been. It was only distributed in the UK and to certain restricted areas at that. Secondly, the quality of both the work and the publication needed much improvement. In my personal opinion, both were below the required standard. Thirdly, the issues discussed in the booklet were only tackled in light of the Ḥanafī school of Islamic law, for the book was mainly directed at those who follow this school. Finally, many contemporary issues, such as the taking of the morning-after pill, the use of the loop, selling contraceptives, the role of doctors with regard to abortion, were not discussed.

In order to rectify these shortcomings, I felt it necessary to revise the book and improve on the earlier work. Thus, in the name of Allāh Almighty, I began working on it and to my amazement and through the sheer grace of Allāh Most High, the work was virtually transformed into a completely new book. I have included many things that were not covered and excluded other unessential aspects. Some parts of the book were modified, altered, and made more reader-friendly.

To further the benefit of the book, references for all the quotes were added, citing volume, page, and ḥadīth numbers. Similarly, notes explaining key terms and concepts were included wherever necessary.

I hope this work sheds some light on the very important issues of contraception and abortion. I have tried my utmost to explain issues in a systematic and simplified manner without unnecessary complication. May Allāh Most High accept this humble effort and make it purely for His sake. *Āmīn.*

I would like to thank all those who assisted me in any way in the publication of this work. I am grateful to my parents, who inspired me to take the path of seeking sacred knowledge; all my teachers, who are the main reason for this work being possible; my wife, who gave me support and allowed me the freedom, peace, and tranquility in which to write; and all my family, friends, and associates, especially those at

White Thread Press who assisted in editing, typesetting, and otherwise laboring admirably to bring this work to fruition. May Allāh Most High reward all of them abundantly and may He give us success and guide us all. *Āmīn.*

Muhammad ibn Adam al-Kawthari
Darul Iftaa, Leicester, UK
Ramaḍān 22, 1425 | November 5, 2004

Introduction

Birth control, or family planning through contraception, has become a common practice in society. Recently, many new methods of permanent and temporary contraception have become widespread, and consequently Muslims are also increasingly adopting the various means of limiting or spacing out procreation.

The need to practice birth control arises due to many reasons: physical weakness, health concerns, fear of poverty, spacing out children in order to give them adequate attention, and other similar reasons. Prior to dealing with the Islamic viewpoint with regard to birth control, the purpose and objective of marriage within the Islamic context needs to be fully understood.

The Purpose of Marriage

There is no doubt that birth control, in general, is contrary to the spirit of Islamic teachings. It contradicts one of the primary and foremost objectives of marriage, which is procreation. Islam encourages its followers to procreate in order to increase the Umma (nation) of Allāh's Messenger ﷺ. Allāh Most High says in the Qur'ān:

﴿فَالْآنَ بَاشِرُوهُنَّ وَابْتَغُوا مَا كَتَبَ اللَّهُ لَكُمْ﴾

So now have relations with them (your wives) and seek what Allāh has ordained for you (Qur'ān 2:187).

The great exegete (*mufassir*) of the Qur'ān, Imām Ibn Kathīr (may Allāh have mercy on him) quotes from many great Companions (*ṣaḥāba*), their followers (*tābiʿūn*), and other classical exegetes (*mufassirūn*), such as Abū Hurayra, ʿAbdullāh ibn ʿAbbās, Anas, Mujāhid, ʿIkrima, Saʿīd ibn Jubayr, and others ☙, that the words of Allāh Most High "and seek" refers to having children (*Tafsīr al-Qur'ān al-ʿAẓīm* 1:300).

One of the great nineteenth century scholars of Qur'ānic exegesis and Prophetic narrations in the Indian Subcontinent, ʿAllāma Shabbīr Aḥmad ʿUthmānī (may Allāh have mercy on him), writes in his renowned Urdu exegesis of the Qur'ān,

> You should seek the children ordained for you in the Heavenly Book (*Al-Lawḥ al-maḥfūẓ*) through intercourse with your women. Mere satisfaction of lust and sexual desire should not be the aim. This verse also alludes to the undesirable nature of ʿazl [contraceptive method practiced during the Messenger of Allāh's time, known as coitus interruptus] and the prohibition of sodomy" (*Tafsīr ʿUthmānī* 32).

Sayyiduna Maʿqil ibn Yasār ☙ narrates that a man came to the Messenger of Allāh ☙ and said, "I have found a woman of rank and beauty, but she is not able to give birth to children. Should I marry her? The Messenger of Allāh ☙ said, "No." He came to him again, but he still refused. He came to him the third time and the Messenger of Allāh ☙ said,

تزوَّجوا الودود الولود فإني مُكاثِر بكم

Marry women who are loving and fertile, for with you I shall outnumber [other nations] (*Abū Dāwūd* 2043, *Nasāʾī* 1966).

Mullā ʿAlī al-Qārī (may Allāh have mercy on him), the great Ḥanafī jurist and ḥadīth expert, states while explaining the above ḥadīth, "When a loving woman fails to procreate, the aim and purpose of marriage, which is to increase the size of the Umma, will not be achieved. These two qualities (love and procreation) can be identified in virgins by looking at her close relatives, for closely related people are similar to one another in nature" (*Mirqāt al-Mafātīḥ Sharḥ Mishkāt al-Maṣābīḥ* 6:192).

ʿUwaym ibn Sāʿida al-Anṣārī ⬥ narrates from his father, who narrates from his father, that the Messenger of Allāh ⬥ said,

عليكم بالأبكار، فإنهن أعْذبُ أفواهًا، وأنتقُ أرحامًا، وأرْضى باليسير

Marry virgins, for they have sweeter mouths, more productive wombs, and are more easily satisfied with little (*Ibn Māja* 1861 and recorded by Imām Suyūṭī in his *Al-Jāmiʿ al-Ṣaghīr*).

The above does not in any way conclude that one should not marry non-virgins. The Messenger of Allāh ⬥ himself married many non-virgin women. His beloved first wife Sayyida Khadīja ⬥ was not only a non-virgin, but much older than him, too. As such, there is nothing wrong whatsoever Islamically in marrying non-virgin women and widows.

Sayyida ʿĀʾisha ⬥ narrates that the Messenger of Allāh ⬥ said,

النكاح من سُنَّتي، فمن لم يعمل بسُنَّتي فليس مني، و تزوَّجوا فإني مُكاثر بكم الأمم

Marriage is from my way (Sunna), thus whosoever does not practice my way [out of rejection] is not from me. And marry [and procreate], for indeed I will outnumber the other nations by you (*Ibn Māja* 1846).

It is clearly evident from the aforementioned texts of the Qurʾān and Sunna that procreation is one of the main objectives of marriage (along with the other aims and objectives, such as saving one's self from fornication and the unlawful, guarding one's modesty, and enjoying the company of one's spouse). The Messenger of Allāh ⬥ has encouraged us to marry in order to seek what Allāh provides through the beautiful union of a man and woman. As such, Muslims can never look favorably upon practicing birth control for the sake of avoiding pregnancy.

Besides, a large family unit becomes a means of protection and an asset in times of need. It teaches one to be responsible, to love and cherish the other members of the family, and to care for and share with one another. These are just some of the reasons Islam encourages procreation.

It should be noted that emphasis has been laid here on procreation for the obvious reason that this book is dealing with matters relating to it. However, one must not overlook the other very important objectives of marriage. We should also keep in mind not to look down upon those who are not fortunate enough to have children. It is the wisdom of Allāh Most High that He bestows some people with children and not others. Islam teaches us that the creation of life is the exclusive function of Allāh Most High. No matter what method and means one employs, if Allāh Almighty does not wish to grant children, one will never have children. Allāh Most High says:

> To Allāh belongs the dominion of the heavens and the earth. He creates what He wills. He bestows female (children) to whomsoever He wills and bestows male (children) to whomsoever He wills, or He bestows both males and females, and He leaves barren whomsoever He wills. He is full of Knowledge and Power (Qur'ān 42:49–50).

Islamic Upbringing: An Important Responsibility

However, it is worth mentioning that the goal is not simply to produce any child that will live in the next generation; rather, it is to instill in children righteous and pious attitudes and to raise children who will be obedient to Allāh Most High and who will be a source of reward for their parents after they die.

Sayyiduna Abū Hūrayra ﵁ narrates that the Messenger of Allāh ﷺ said,

إذا مات الإنسانُ انقطع عنه عمَلُه إلا من ثلاثة، إلا من صدقة جاريَة، أو علم يُنتفع به، أو ولدٍ صالح يدعو له

> When a human being dies, his actions [good deeds] come to an end except for three: a continuing charity, knowledge [that one left behind] from which others benefit, and a righteous child who supplicates for him (*Ṣaḥīḥ Muslim* 1631).

The Messenger of Allāh ﷺ will not be priding himself before the other nations on the Day of Judgment (Qiyāma) on the children of Muslim parents who left the path of Islam. Thus, it is the responsibility of Muslim parents that their children have an Islamic upbringing and that they be given moral, spiritual, and physical training. Allāh Most High says in His Book:

﴿يَا أَيُّهَا الَّذِيْنَ آمَنُوْا قُوْا أَنفُسَكُمْ وَأَهْلِيْكُمْ نَارًا وَقُودُهَا النَّاسُ وَالْحِجَارَةُ﴾

> O you who believe! Save yourselves and your families from a fire whose fuel is men and stones (Qur'ān 66:6).

Children: A Source of Mercy for the Parents

Children are one of the tremendous favors of Allāh Most High. He has made the child a source of good and mercy for its parents in all situations. If he lives longer than his parents, he will benefit them by supplicating for them and seeking forgiveness for them, as we have seen in the ḥadīth of Abū Hurayra ﷺ quoted earlier. On the other hand, if the child unfortunately dies before the parents, then the child will intercede for them and be a means of their entering paradise.

Sayyiduna Abū Saʿīd al-Khudrī ﷺ narrates that on one occasion women requested the Messenger of Allāh ﷺ to allocate for them a day wherein he could advise them. So he fixed a day for them and on one occasion said,

أَيُّمَا امْرَأَةٍ مَاتَ لَهَا ثَلَاثَةٌ مِنَ الوَلَدِ، كَانُوْا لَهَا حِجَابًا مِنَ النَّارِ. قَالَتِ امْرَأَةٌ: وَاثْنَانِ، قَالَ: وَاثْنَانِ

> Any woman who has three children who all die, they will be a shield for

her from the Hellfire. A woman said, "And two?" He replied, "And two" (*Bukhārī* 1192, *Muslim* 2634).

Sayyiduna Abū Hurayra ☙ narrates that the Messenger of Allāh ﷺ said,

صِغَارُهم دعامِيصُ الجنَّة يتلقَّى أحدهم أباه (أو قال أبويه) فيأخذ بثوبه (أو قال بيده)
كما آخذ أنا بصَنِفَة ثوبك هذا، فلا يتناهى (أو قال فلا ينتهي) حتى يُدخله الله وأباه الجنة

Their young children will roam freely in paradise. When one of them meets his father (or he said, his parents) he will take hold of [the edge of] his garment (or he said, his hand) just as I am now taking hold of the edge of your garment, and not let go until Allāh admits him and his father into paradise (*Muslim* 2635).

The few Qur'ānic verses and ḥadīths quoted above clearly indicate that Islam encourages us to have children, for they are a gift to us from Allāh Most High. Just ask those who are unable to have children what they would do or give in order to have a child of their own. This does not imply, however, that practicing birth control is absolutely unlawful in Islam, as we will see further along, but it does illustrate what Islam really thinks about procreation.

Muslims who call for population control must realize that they are openly contradicting one of the main objectives of marriage. The aim of population control is to curtail increases in the population by reducing the birth rate. China is a classic example of where this practice has been highly encouraged by the government to the extent that families face financial and other consequences if they exceed government "recommendations." In the US, the term population control is not recognized, because it denotes the idea of forced birth control; rather, preference is given to the term "population education"—talking to families about overpopulation in the hope that they will make responsible decisions regarding family sizes. It is argued that although it is every family's right to have as many children as they wish, it is also in everyone's "best interest" to help curb population growth.

The main drive for this practice is the fear of there not being enough resources in the world to cater for increases in population—in particular, a want of food (known as the Malthusian catastrophe) and of clean water, shelter, warmth, and arable land. Islam regards children as a source of mercy, compassion, and coolness for one's eyes, while movements for population control call for halting the birth of children on account of insecurities arising from their sheer lack of belief and trust in Allāh Most High. As Muslims, we know that all sustenance is from Allāh Most High and that He alone is the Provider for all our needs. To follow and adopt such a method for the reason outlined goes against the very core of our belief. A Muslim aware of the exhortations in Sharīʿa regarding procreation can never look with favor upon or take part in any call for population control.

Birth Control In Islamic Law

We can now move on to discuss the Islamic viewpoint on the various aspects of birth control. Birth control and contraception can be primarily divided into two categories: (1) Irreversible (or permanent) contraception and (2) Reversible (or temporary) contraception.

Irreversible Contraception

When a couple decides to permanently forgo conceiving any children, they often opt for a sterilization operation. Normally, there are two types of sterilization operations, one performed on the male and the other on the female:

Male Sterilization (Vasectomy)
This is a quick operation performed on the male, which can be done under localized anesthesia. Two little incisions are made at the top of the scrotum, and the duct on each side that carries the sperm to the outside is severed.

Female Sterilization (Tubal Ligation or Tubectomy)
This operation involves cutting, tying, clipping, or blocking the fallopian tube, thus keeping the sperm and egg apart and preventing fertilization. This renders a woman incapable of ever having children again.

ISLAMIC VIEWPOINT ON IRREVERSIBLE CONTRACEPTION

Under normal circumstances, irreversible contraception, whether it is in the form of a vasectomy or tubectomy, is absolutely and decidedly prohibited (*ḥarām*) in Islam and cannot be sanctioned, for it clearly contradicts the teachings of Sharīʿa.

Islamic law also prohibits castration. A common factor between vasectomy and castration is that both destroy the power of reproduction in a man, although the ability to cohabit still exists in both. Sayyiduna Saʿd ibn Abī Waqqās ؓ relates,

رَدَّ رسول الله صلى الله عليه و سلم على عثمانَ بن مَظعون التَّبَتُّل، ولو أذِنَ له لاخْتصينا

The Messenger of Allāh ﷺ forbade ʿUthmān ibn Maẓʿūn ؓ from abstaining from marriage. If he had allowed him, we would have castrated ourselves (*Bukhārī* 4786, *Muslim* 1402).

Sayyiduna ʿAbdullāh ibn Masʿūd ؓ says,

كنّا نَغْزو مع رسول الله صلى الله عليه وسلم وليس لنا شيءٌ، فقلنا ألا نَسْتخصي؟ فنهانا عن ذلك

We used to be engaged in *jihād* with the Messenger of Allāh ﷺ and we had no one [with whom we could fulfill our desires]. So we asked if we could get ourselves castrated. The Messenger of Allāh ﷺ forbade us from doing so (*Bukhārī* 4787).

The great ḥadīth expert and Shāfiʿī jurist (*faqīh*) Imām Nawawī (may Allāh have mercy on him) states in his monumental commentary of

Imām Muslim's *Ṣaḥīḥ,* while explaining the ḥadīth of ʿUthmān ibn Maẓʿūn ﵁ quoted above, "The statement, 'If the Messenger of Allāh ﷺ had allowed him to abstain from marrying, we would have got ourselves castrated,' indicates that some of the Companions ﵃ were under the impression, according to their own understanding (*ijtihād*), that castration was permissible. However, this understanding of theirs was not correct, because castration of humans was deemed unlawful (*ḥarām*), whether one is old or young" (*Al-Minhāj Sharḥ Ṣaḥīḥ Muslim ibn al-Ḥajjāj* 1052). These Companions had intended to resort to castration to free themselves completely for the worship of Allāh Most High and serve Islam.

The renowned ḥadīth master and Ḥanafī jurist Imām Badr al-Dīn al-ʿAynī (may Allāh have mercy on him) states in his commentary of *Ṣaḥīḥ al-Bukhārī,* quoting from Imām Qurṭubī, "Castration is to cut the organs of the body that are the basis for offspring. There is a lot of pain in getting castrated and could even lead to death. It is considered to be unlawful (*ḥarām*) by the consensus of all the scholars" (*ʿUmdat al-Qārī* 14:14).

The prominent Ḥanafī jurist Imām Ḥaskafī (may Allāh have mercy on him) states, "As for the castration of humans, it is unlawful (*ḥarām*)" (*Radd al-Muḥtār ʿala 'l-Durr al-Mukhtār* 6:3888).

Furthermore, castration is also considered to be a form of mutilation of one's body (*muthla*), which has also been categorically forbidden in the Sharīʿa. Allāh Most High mentions in Sūrat al-Nisā' the words of Satan, when he said:

﴿وَلَأُضِلَّنَّهُمْ وَلَأُمَنِّيَنَّهُمْ وَلَآمُرَنَّهُمْ فَلَيُبَتِّكُنَّ آذَانَ الْأَنْعَامِ وَلَآمُرَنَّهُمْ فَلَيُغَيِّرُنَّ خَلْقَ اللّٰهِ﴾

> I will mislead them, and I will create in them false desires; I will order them to slit the ears of cattle and to deface the (fair) nature created by Allāh (Qur'ān 4:119).

To deface the fair nature created by Allāh Most High both physically and spiritually, is what Satan likes and orders to practice.

These and other texts (of the Sunna and works of classical scholars) clearly show the impermissibility of castration, which in effect is a form of sterilization. It is true that many of the irreversible contraceptive methods are unlike castration, but the similarity between them is apparent. Castration involves removing the testicles, hence rendering one permanently incapable of producing children. The various methods of irreversible contraception are no different, in that they permanently prevent one from procreating. Thus, irreversible contraception in all its forms is unlawful (*ḥarām*) by drawing an analogy with the Messenger of Allāh's ﷺ prohibition of castration.

Therefore, terminating the ability to procreate, through castration or any other method, is unlawful (*ḥarām*) by the consensus (*ijmāᶜ*) of all the scholars. To undergo a vasectomy, tubectomy, or any other method of irreversible contraception and to be permanently deprived of the means of procreation simply out of selfishness or personal convenience is indeed ingratitude toward the Creator of this most precious gift. A Muslim aware of the exhortations and advice of the Messenger of Allāh ﷺ regarding procreation can never consider any such method that will restrict this process.

Sterilization in Dire Situations

Despite the extreme and severe nature of sterilization and irreversible contraception, scholars mention that it is permitted in cases of absolute necessity. The famous principles of Islamic jurisprudence based on the teachings of the Qur'ān and Sunna permit the use of unlawful things in cases of utter necessity (*ḍarūra*). In such situations, certain prohibitions are waived, as when the prohibition of eating carrion and drinking wine is suspended when the life of a person is threatened.

The well-known principle of Islamic jurisprudence based on the guidelines of the Qur'ān and Sunna states, "Necessities make prohibitions lawful" (*Al-Ashbāh wa 'l-Naẓā'ir* 85).

At times, a woman's health—or worse, her life—is threatened by pregnancy. Some women are incapable of giving birth naturally, while others, after giving birth two or three times through a Caesarean operation, face the risk of losing their life with additional births.

Thus, if, after taking unbiased and professional medical advice from an experienced Muslim doctor, one comes to the conclusion that the life or permanent health of a woman would be seriously affected by a pregnancy and that there is no other cure for her illness, only then would female sterilization (tubectomy) be permissible.[1]

Reversible Contraception

Some reversible contraceptive methods prevent pregnancy by creating a barrier between the sperm cells and egg, while others either stop the fertilized egg from developing or induce the woman's body to discard her eggs even after fertilization. There are various methods of practicing reversible contraception, of which the major ones are mentioned below. The Islamic viewpoint on all of these will be mentioned further on.

Coitus Interruptus (ʿazl)

This is a physical method where the man withdraws his sexual organ from his spouse's genitals just before ejaculation. It is also referred to as "coitus interruptus," "outside ejaculation," or "the withdrawal method." In the Arabic language and in the various texts of ḥadīth and works of

1 Note that the jurists normally permit availing of unlawful medication or treatment (in cases of necessity) provided one is advised by a qualified, upright Muslim doctor. The reason is that a God-fearing Muslim doctor would normally be mindful of the rules of Sharīʿa and of accountability in the Hereafter; hence, the doctor would not hasten in advising the Muslim patient to do something unlawful unless there is a genuine need. However, it will be permitted to take the opinion of a non-Muslim doctor if it confirms one's past experience with an upright Muslim doctor in a similar situation. Likewise, if there is no reasonable Muslim doctor available, it would be permitted to take medical advice from non-Muslim doctors after they have been made aware of the Islamic rulings and they can be generally trusted to give sound advice with these in mind.

classical scholars, it is known as *ʿazl.* It was a common method of contraception during the era of Allāh's Messenger ﷺ. For simplicity, I will use the terms coitus interruptus and *ʿazl* in our discussion.

The Rhythm Method

Another physical method of contraception is known as the rhythm method or the periodic practice of abstinence. This method is based on abstention from intercourse during the time of the month when the woman is most likely to conceive. This occurs around the time a woman ovulates, which is usually fourteen days prior to the onset of her period. As the sperm can survive between three to seven days in the body and the egg can remain fertile in the fallopian tubes and vagina for up to three days as well, a couple must abstain from intercourse for three to five days prior to and after ovulation. The woman can calculate her ovulation date by careful monitoring on a calendar or by recording her basal body temperature each month, as her body temperature will rise two days prior to ovulation.

Intra-Uterine Devices (IUD)

Intra-uterine devices are mechanical means of contraception often described as the loop, the coil, or the curl. They are inserted into the woman's vagina and normally prevent a fertilized egg from implanting itself into the womb.

Condoms

A condom is a tube of fine latex closed at one end and worn by the man on his sexual organ during intercourse. When the man ejaculates, the condom retains the semen, thereby preventing it from reaching the woman's womb. There are also female condoms available. A female condom is a soft, loose-fitting plastic pouch that lines the vagina. It has a soft ring at each end. The ring at the closed end is used to put the device inside the vagina and hold it in place. The other ring stays outside the vagina and partly covers the labia area. Female condoms are widely available without prescription and are intended to be worn by women during sexual intercourse in order to help prevent pregnancy.

Diaphragms and Caps

These are round dome-shaped contraceptives made of latex that are inserted into the vagina of the woman and cover the cervix, preventing any sperm from entering the womb.

Oral Contraceptive Pills

The pill contains two hormones called estrogen and progesterone, both of which occur naturally in the body. It works by preventing the release of the egg each month. The pill has revolutionized contraception, and according to a survey, three million women in Britain take the pill every day. In the United States, the pill and female sterilization have been the two leading contraceptive methods since 1982, with a record 30.6% of users taking the pill in 2002, according to one survey. That calculates out to 11,661 women—the highest number of users for this method of contraception in comparison to all other methods.

Injections

It is possible to provide three months protection from pregnancy by an intra-muscular injection of progesterone.

Locally Acting Spermicidal Jellies

Spermicidal jellies create a virtual barrier between the man's sperm and the woman's egg. They contain chemicals that kill the sperm cells when they come into contact with them.

Islamic Viewpoint on Reversible Contraception

As mentioned earlier, the contraceptive method practiced by the Arabs during the lifetime of the Messenger of Allāh ﷺ was that of coitus interruptus (*ʿazl*). Thus, it is imperative that we understand the Islamic ruling with regards to *ʿazl,* for most of the other contemporary reversible contraceptive methods generally have the same ruling as *ʿazl.*

By looking into the Sunna literature, it becomes clear that the Messenger of Allāh ﷺ neither outright prohibited *ʿazl* nor permitted it categorically. This view is derived from the following Prophetic narrations:

عن جابر قال: كنَّا نَعزلُ على عهد النبي صلى الله عليه و سلم والقرآنُ ينزل

Sayyiduna Jābir ؓ said, "We used to practice coitus interruptus during the time the Qur'ān was being revealed" (*Bukhārī* 4911, *Muslim* 1440).

عن جابر قال: كنا نعزلُ على عهد رسول الله صلى الله عليه وسلم، فبلغ ذلك نبيَّ الله صلى الله عليه وسلم، فلم يَنهَنا

Sayyiduna Jābir ؓ says, "We used to practice coitus interruptus during the lifetime of the Messenger of Allāh ﷺ. The Prophet of Allāh ﷺ came to know of it and he did not forbid us from practicing it" (*Muslim* 1440).

عن أبي سعيد الخُدْري قال: كنا نعزل، فسألنا رسول الله صلى الله عليه وسلم فقال: أوَ إنكم لتفعلون – قالها ثلاثا – ما من نسَمَة كائنةٍ إلى يوم القيامة إلا هي كائنة

Sayyiduna Abū Saʿid al-Khudrī ؓ said, "We used to practice coitus interruptus. So we asked the Messenger of Allāh ﷺ about it and he said, 'So you really practice it?' He said this thrice, then said, 'There is no soul that is destined to exist but will come into existence, until the Day of Judgment'" (*Bukhārī* 4912).

عن ابن مُحَيْريز أنه قال: دخلتُ أنا وأبو صِرْمة على أبي سعيد الخدري، فسأله أبو صرمة فقال: يا أبا سعيد، هل سمعتَ رسول الله صلى الله عليه و سلم يذكر العزل؟ فقال: نعم، غزوْنا مع رسول الله صلى الله عليه و سلم غزوة بالمُصطلق، . . . فقلنا: نعزل ورسول الله صلى الله عليه و سلم بين أظهُرنا لا نسأله، فسألنا رسول الله صلى الله عليه وسلم، فقال: لا، عليكم أن لا تفعلوا، ما كتب الله خلْق نسَمَة هي كائنة إلى يوم القيامة إلا ستكون

Ibn Muḥayrīz narrates that he and Abū Ṣirma visited Abū Saʿīd al-Khudrī ﷺ, and Abū Ṣirma asked Abū Saʿīd al-Khudrī, "O Abū Saʿīd, did you hear the Messenger of Allāh ﷺ mentioning coitus interruptus?" He said, "Yes, we went out with the Messenger of Allāh ﷺ on an expedition to the Banū Muṣṭaliq. . . . We said, 'We are practicing *ʿazl* while the Messenger of Allāh ﷺ is among us; why not ask him?' Thus, we asked the Messenger of Allāh ﷺ, and he said, 'It does not matter if you do not practice it, for every soul that is to be born up to the Day of Resurrection will be born'" (*Muslim* 1438).

The meaning of the Messenger of Allāh's statement: "It does not matter if you do not practice it" is that there is no discernible difference in practicing *ʿazl* or abstaining from it, because whatever Allāh has pre-determined will surely occur. Every soul that is destined to be born will surely be born whether one practices *ʿazl* or otherwise. Similarly, every soul that Allāh has not destined to create will not be born, so there is no real benefit in practicing *ʿazl* (*Al-Minhāj Sharḥ Ṣaḥīḥ Muslim ibn al-Ḥajjāj*).

عن أبي سعيد الخدري قال: ذكر العزل عند رسول الله صلى الله عليه و سلم، فقال: ولِمَ يفعلُ ذلك أحدكم؟ (ولم يقل: فلا يفعلْ ذلك أحدكم) فإنه ليست نفسٌ مخلوقة إلا الله خالقها

Sayyiduna Abū Saʿīd al-Khudrī ﷺ narrates, "The practice of coitus interruptus was mentioned in the presence of the Messenger of Allāh ﷺ, upon which he said, "Why does one of you practice it? (He did not say, 'You should not practice it') for there is no soul created but that Allāh is its Creator" (*Muslim* 1438).

عن أبي الوداك عن أبي سعيد الخدري سمعه يقول: سئل رسول الله صلى الله عليه و سلم عن العزل؟ فقال: ما من كلِّ الماء يكون الولدُ، وإذا أراد الله خلْقَ شيء لم يمنعْه شيء

Sayyiduna Abū Saʿīd al-Khudrī ﷺ narrates that the Messenger of Allāh ﷺ was asked about *ʿazl*, upon which he said, "The child is not born from all the liquid (semen), and when Allāh intends to create something, nothing can prevent Him" (*Muslim* 1438).

In this narration, the same message is being given, namely, that even if one intends to prevent the occurrence of pregnancy by practicing coitus interruptus, it only takes a drop of semen for the woman to conceive. Thus, if Allāh wills for a child to be born, nothing can prevent His will, including the practice of ʿazl.

عن جابر أن رجلا أتى رسول الله صلى الله عليه وسلم فقال: إن لي جارية، هي خادمُنا وسانيتنا، وأنا أطوف عليها وأنا أكره أن تحمِل، فقال: اِعزلْ عنها إن شئت، فإنه سيأتيها ما قُدِّر لها فلبِث الرجل، ثم أتاه فقال: إن الجارية قد حبلتْ، فقال: قد أخبرتك أنه سيأتيها ما قُدِّر لها

Sayyidunā Jābir ☙ narrates that a man came to the Messenger of Allāh 🌸 and said, "I have a slave girl who is our servant that carries water for us, and I have relations with her, but I do not want her to conceive?" He 🌸 said, "Practice ʿazl if you wish, for she will receive what has been predetermined for her." The man remained [practicing ʿazl for a while] and then came to the Messenger of Allāh 🌸 and said, "The slave girl has become pregnant." The Messenger of Allāh 🌸 said, "I told you that she will receive what has been predetermined for her" (*Muslim* 1439).

In some of the above ḥadīths, the practice of ʿazl (and reversible contraception in general) is neither explicitly prohibited nor permitted. The narrations wherein the Messenger of Allāh 🌸 says "Why does one of you practice it?" and "So you really practice it" and "It does not matter if you do not practice it, for every soul that is to be born up to the Day of Resurrection will be born" indicate that the Messenger of Allāh 🌸 did not prohibit this practice.

The first two narrations along with the last narration of Sayyidunā Jābir ☙ seem to indicate that the practice of ʿazl is permissible. The meaning of "we used to practice ʿazl while the Qurʾān was being revealed" is that although we practice this, no revelation was sent to the Messenger of Allāh 🌸 ordering us to abstain from it.

It is a well-established principle of Islamic jurisprudence that if the

Messenger of Allāh ﷺ remained silent on an ongoing practice, this is an indication of its permissibility, for the Messenger of Allāh ﷺ must, by the Sharīʿa, disapprove of something that is wrong or unlawful.[2]

Similarly, in the last narration, the Messenger of Allāh ﷺ evidently permitted this practice. The statement of the Messenger of Allāh ﷺ "Practice ʿazl if you wish, for she will receive what has been predetermined for her" clearly permits practicing ʿazl.

However, the objection arises because there is one ḥadīth that seems to denote the impermissibility of practicing ʿazl.

عن جدامة بنت وهب، أختِ عكاشة، قالت حضرتُ رسول الله رسول الله صلى الله عليه وسلم في أناسٍ، وهو يقول: لقد هممتُ أن أنهى عن الغِيلَة، فنظرتُ في الرُّوم وفارس، فإذا هم يغيلون أولادهم، فلا يضرُّ أولادَهم ذلك شيئا. ثم سألوه عن العزل؟ فقال رسول الله صلى الله عليه و سلم: ذلك الوأْدُ الخفيُّ

Judāma bint Wahb ☙, the sister of ʿUkāsha, says, "I was present with a group of people when the Messenger of Allāh ﷺ said, 'I considered prohibiting sexual intercourse during the period of breastfeeding (*ghayla*), but I observed the Byzantines and Persians practice this, and their children were not harmed.' Then they [the Companions] asked him regarding coitus interruptus and he said, 'That is hidden infanticide' [i.e., a lesser degree of infanticide]." One of the reporters of this ḥadīth, ʿUbaydullāh, added, narrating from Muqrī, "This act is also to be included

---

2 Books on the Principles of Islamic jurisprudence (*uṣūl al-fiqh*) and ḥadīth (*uṣūl al-ḥadīth*) have elaborated on this topic. In a nutshell, acts and sayings of the Companions that came to the knowledge of the Messenger of Allāh ﷺ and were neither approved nor disapproved of by him, but elicited nothing more than a reply of silence, falls under the category of the tacitly approved sunna (*sunna taqrīriyya*), thus indicating permissibility. An example of this is when one of the prominent Companions, ʿAmr ibn-ʿĀṣ (Allāh be pleased with him), narrated that in the campaign of Dhāt al-Salāsil he had a wet dream in the night, but owing to extreme cold did not take an obligatory ritual bath but instead performed Fajr prayer with dry ablution (*tayammum*). He then related this to the Messenger of Allāh ﷺ stating that Allāh Almighty forbids one to kill oneself. The Messenger of Allāh ﷺ upon hearing this smiled, but said nothing, which would imply that *tayammum* is permissible in similar circumstances, that is, when extreme cold proves to be hazardous to one's health (see Hashim Kamali, *Principles of Islamic Jurisprudence* 50–51).

in the Qur'ānic verse, 'And when the girl buried alive is asked as for what reason she was murdered'" (Qur'ān 81:8–9) (*Muslim* 1442).[3]

This narration of Judāma bint Wahb al-Asadiyya ﵂, recorded by Imām Muslim in his *Ṣaḥīḥ,* clearly indicates the impermissibility of practicing *ʿazl,* because the Messenger of Allāh ﷺ regarded it as a hidden form of the pre-Islamic (*jāhiliyya*) practice of female infanticide.

Hence, scholars of ḥadīth (*muḥaddithūn*) have attempted, by going in great depth, to resolve the apparent contradiction between this narration of Judāma (which likens *ʿazl* to female infanticide) and the other narrations (which indicate its permissibility).

Some scholars regarded the ḥadīth of Judāma bint Wahb to be weak (*ḍaʿīf*) because it contradicts a large number of authentic narrations on the issue. Others considered it to be abrogated (*mansūkh*), while some scholars preferred it above all the other narrations (*Fatḥ al-Bārī* 9:383).

Mullā ʿAlī al-Qārī (may Allāh have mercy on him) comments while explaining this ḥadīth of Judāma bint Wahb, "This ḥadīth does not denote the unlawfulness of practicing *ʿazl.* Rather, it indicates that it is disliked (*makrūh*), because by practicing *ʿazl,* there does not result any actual taking of life but only something somewhat similar to it" (*Mirqāt al-Mafātīḥ* 6:238).

One of the renowned Ḥanafī jurists of recent times in the Indian Subcontinent, Muftī Muḥammad Shafīʿ ʿUthmānī (Allāh have mercy

---

3 It must be mentioned here that there is another narration recorded by Imām Tirmidhī in his *Sunan* wherein the Messenger of Allāh ﷺ was asked about the Jews who said that *ʿazl* was a minor infanticide. The Messenger of Allāh ﷺ categorically denied such a contention, saying that the Jews had lied. He added: "If Allāh wills its creation you cannot stop Him" (*Tirmidhī* 1136). There is no concrete contradiction between the two ḥadīths, for there is a difference between "hidden infanticide" (*wa'd al-khafī*) and "minor infanticide" (*maw'ūda ṣughrā*). The Jews regarded the practice of *ʿazl* to be one of the forms of infanticide and actual murder, so they said that it was "minor infanticide." The Messenger of Allāh ﷺ criticized the Jews for having this belief and stated that they were wrong. However, the Messenger ﷺ himself (in this narration of Judāma) considered it to be "hidden infanticide"—not that it is an actual form of infanticide that can be considered murder, but that the intention is similar to that of infanticide, which is to prevent additional children. That is why it is called "hidden infanticide" (see Ibn Ḥajr al-ʿAsqalānī, "Bāb al-ʿAzl" in *Fatḥ al-Bārī* 9:384).

on him), has beautifully reconciled the various ḥadīths and summarized this in his Urdu treatise *Ḍabt-i Wilādat.* He states, "The scholars have given various explanations by which the difference in the above narrations can be reconciled. However, the most clear and acceptable explanation is that the ḥadīth of Judāma (in which *ʿazl* was considered to be hidden infanticide) should be interpreted to indicate the undesirable nature of this practice, and the remaining narrations be interpreted to establish its permissibility. Thus, taking all these narrations into account, it can be concluded that the practice of *ʿazl* is permissible although somewhat disliked (*makrūh tanzīhan*)" (*Ḍabt-i Wilādat* 18).

We may conclude from this that practicing coitus interruptus and thus, by extension, other forms of reversible contraception is permissible but somewhat disliked (*makrūh tanzīhan*). This is the view taken by many Companions ﷺ and the scholars of the four major Sunnī schools of Islamic law (but see page 44 for Mālikī prohibition of the pill).

The Ḥanafī School

The majority view in the Ḥanafī school is that practicing *ʿazl* and other reversible contraceptive methods is in itself permitted but somewhat disliked and discouraged.

Imām Ḥaskafī (may Allāh have mercy on him), a prominent jurist of this school, states in his *Al-Durr al-Mukhtār,* "It is permissible to practice *ʿazl* with a woman with her consent, although it is stated in [*Fatāwā*] *Khāniya* that it is permissible even without the wife's consent in our times due to religious decline."

Imām Ibn ʿĀbidīn (may Allāh have mercy on him), a later authority in the Ḥanafī school, states while commenting on the above statement of Ḥaskafī, "Imām Ibn al-Kamāl states [in his *Fatḥ al-Qadīr*] that if there is a fear of begetting delinquent and mischievous children, it will be permitted to practice *ʿazl* with a woman even without her consent" (*Radd al-Muḥtār ʿala 'l-Durr al-Mukhtār* 3:175–176).

He further states, "Thus, it becomes known from what has been mentioned in *Khāniya* that the transmitted position in the (Ḥanafī) school is that *ʿazl* is not permitted without the wife's consent and approval, but this dispensation (of not seeking her permission) is given by some jurists in certain situations and at certain times. . . . Quhistānī states, 'This [the need for the wife's consent] is when the husband does not fear any evil on the child due to "bad times." Otherwise it is allowed even without her permission.' Also, similar to the excuse of fearing evil on the child is the couple undertaking a lengthy and difficult journey, or the couple being in enemy lands (*dār al-ḥarb*) and fearing for their child's safety, or the wife being morally corrupt and the husband intending to separate from her without conceiving any more children" (ibid.).

Imām Kamāl ibn al-Humām (may Allāh have mercy on him) states in his *Fatḥ al-Qadīr*, "Coitus interruptus is generally permissible according to the majority of scholars. Some Companions ﷺ and other scholars regarded it to be disliked based on the narration of Judāma recorded by Imām Muslim in his *Ṣaḥīḥ*. However, the correct opinion is that it is permissible because of the many ḥadīths mentioned in this regard" (*Fatḥ al-Qadīr* 3:400–401).

Imām Kāsānī (may Allāh have mercy on him) states, "It is prohibitively disliked (*makrūh*) to practice *ʿazl* with one's wife without her consent, for sexual intercourse with ejaculation is a cause of begetting children, and she has a right to have children. . . . However, if *ʿazl* is practiced with her consent, it will not be disliked, for she has agreed to relinquish her right" (*Badāʾiʿ al-Ṣanāʾiʿ* 2:334).

The upshot of the above is that *ʿazl* (and reversible contraception in general) is by and large permissible in the Ḥanafī school with the wife's consent, although slightly disliked. The consent of the spouse is necessary in normal circumstances, and may be overlooked in certain situations, such as the spouse being religiously corrupt, the husband intending to divorce his wife or the wife intending to seek a divorce from her husband, the couple being in hostile territory, and other such situations.

Furthermore, if a reversible form of contraception was practiced for a genuine reason, its undesirability would no longer remain, and it would be totally permissible.

The late Ḥanafī jurist from the Indian Subcontinent, Muftī Muḥammad Shafīʿ ʿUthmānī (may Allāh have mercy on him), drawing from the classical books of Ḥanafī jurisprudence, mentions the valid reasons for practicing reversible contraception in his Urdu work *Ḍabt-i Wilādat.* He says, "It will be acceptable to practice reversible contraception in cases of need such as:

- When a woman is too weak or ill to sustain pregnancy;
- When she is in an area where there is no stability or security;
- When the couple is on a prolonged and difficult journey, in which pregnancy may cause difficulty; and
- When the wife's relationship with her husband is strained and divorce is likely" (*Ḍabt-i Wilādat* 19).

One may add to these:

- Spacing out children in order to give them adequate and equal attention; and
- When the woman is compelled and forced to seek employment due to unavoidable and desperate circumstances. *See* Mujāhid al-Islām Qāsimī, *Birth Control: An Islamic perspective.*

The Mālikī School

Imām Mālik (may Allāh have mercy on him), the founder of the Mālikī school, states explicitly in his renowned ḥadīth collection, *Muwaṭṭā:* "A man should not practice *ʿazl* with his wife except with her permission" (*Muwaṭṭā* 2:112). Imām Ibn Juzay, a Mālikī jurist, states, "Coitus interruptus (*ʿazl*) will not be permissible with one's wife except with her consent" (*Al-Qawānīn al-Fiqhiyya* 160).

The Shāfiʿī School

The Shāfiʿī school is very similar to the Ḥanafī school, in that practicing *ʿazl* and reversible contraception in general is permitted but somewhat disliked.

The renowned jurist of this school, Imām Nawawī (may Allāh have mercy on him), states,

> The early scholars debated as to whether ʿazl was permitted or not. Ibn ʿAbd al-Barr (may Allāh have mercy on him) said that there is no difference of opinion between the scholars in that one should not practice coitus interruptus without the consent of one's wife, for intercourse is a right of hers that she can demand, and sexual intercourse is that which is free from withdrawing and ejaculating outside. It is stated in the majority of the books of our (Shāfiʿī) scholars that it is not permissible to practice ʿazl with a free woman without her consent. This is indicated by the ḥadīth of Sayyiduna ʿUmar ☙, in which he said, "The Messenger of Allāh ☙ forbade the practice of ʿazl with a free woman except with her permission" (as recorded by Aḥmad and Ibn Māja). Imām Ghazālī (may Allāh have mercy on him) said, "Coitus interruptus is permissible, and this is the preferred opinion according to the late [Shāfiʿī] scholars" (*Al-Majmūʿ Sharḥ al-Muhadhdhab* 18:75).

Imām Nawawī (may Allāh have mercy on him) further states in his commentary of *Ṣaḥīḥ Muslim:*

> ʿAzl means to withdraw at the time of ejaculation and to ejaculate outside the vagina. It is a practice that is disliked (*makrūh*) according to us (Shāfiʿīs) at all times, and with all types of women, irrespective of whether she is willing or otherwise, for it leads to a reduction in reproduction. . . . The narrations in this regard have been reconciled with one another, such that the narration signifying the impermissibility of this practice is interpreted to indicate that it is somewhat disliked (*makrūh tanzīhan*), and the narrations indicating its permissibility show that it is not unlawful (*ḥarām*) (*Al-Minhāj Sharḥ Ṣaḥīḥ Muslim* 1085).

Imām Abū Ḥāmid al-Ghazālī (may Allāh have mercy on him) states,

> It is an etiquette of sexual intercourse not to practice coitus interruptus (ʿazl). However if one does, there is disagreement among our [Shāfiʿī]

> scholars as to the permissibility or offensiveness of it, though the correct position according to us is that it is permissible. As for offensiveness (*karāha*), it is a term applied to things that are closer to the unlawful (*ḥarām*), things that are somewhat disliked (and closer to the lawful), and things that merely entail leaving out the superior. *ʿAzl* is considered *makrūh* in the third sense in that it entails leaving out a meritorious act. The meaning of offensiveness (*karāha*) here is merely forgoing a commendable act—that is, to have a child (*Iḥyā ʿUlūm al-Dīn* 2:48).

In conclusion, the Shāfiʿī school regards the practice of *ʿazl*—and, by extension, all other reversible methods of contraception—as somewhat disliked, although permissible in itself. The majority of the school's jurists cite the consent of the wife as a condition for this permissibility.

The Ḥanbalī School

Imām Mardāwī (may Allāh have mercy on him) states, "A man must not practice *ʿazl* without the permission of his wife. . . . This is the relied upon position in the (Ḥanbalī) school and accepted by the majority of the scholars of the school" (*Al-Inṣāf fī Maʿrifat al-Rājiḥ min al-Khilāf* 8:348).

The great Ḥanbalī jurist (*faqīh*) Imām Ibn Qudāma (may Allāh have mercy on him) states,

> *ʿAzl* is disliked (*makrūh*). The meaning of *ʿazl* is to withdraw when ejaculation is imminent and to ejaculate outside the vagina. Its detestability has been narrated from ʿUmar ibn al-Khaṭṭāb, ʿAlī, Ibn ʿUmar, Ibn Masʿūd and also Abū Bakr al-Ṣiddīq ﷺ, for it entails reducing offspring and may well lessen the pleasure [of sex] for a woman . . . . If there is a need to practice it, however, such as when one is fighting in enemy lands (*dār al-ḥarb*) and feels the urge to have sexual relations, then one may cohabit and practice *ʿazl* (*Al-Mughnī* 7:23).

He further states regarding the wife's consent, "It is not permitted to practice *ʿazl* with a woman without her express permission because she has the right to offspring, and [also] because contraception may harm her, so it is not permissible without her permission" (ibid., 7:24).

Conclusion from the Four Schools

By looking at the above texts gathered from the reliable works of the four major Sunnī schools of Islamic law (*madhhabs*), it can be understood that practicing *ʿazl* and reversible contraception in general is, by and large, permissible in all of the four schools with a slight degree of dislike attached to it (but see page 44). This dislike is also removed if and when there is a genuine reason, of which examples have been mentioned.

However, this permissibility of practicing *ʿazl* and reversible contraception hinges on the wife's consent. Most of the schools make this a necessary condition—some strongly and others to a lesser degree. This may even be overlooked in certain situations, as mentioned earlier. Similarly, the wife will also need to seek her husband's permission before employing any method of contraception.

The above is the general ruling with regard to reversible contraception. However, there are certain situations where practicing *ʿazl* and reversible contraception becomes impermissible.

Practicing Contraception for Fear of Poverty

It should be kept in mind that if reversible contraception is practiced for a reason that is contrary to the teachings and principles of the Sharīʿa, it is impermissible. For instance, practicing contraception because of poverty and fear of not being able to adequately provide for a large family is unlawful (*ḥarām*), for Allāh Most High says:

﴿وَمَا مِنْ دَابَّةٍ فِي الْأَرْضِ إِلَّا عَلَى اللَّهِ رِزْقُهَا وَيَعْلَمُ مُسْتَقَرَّهَا وَمُسْتَوْدَعَهَا، كُلٌّ فِي كِتَابٍ مُّبِينٍ﴾

> And there is no moving creature on earth but its sustenance is dependent on Allāh. He knows its resting place and its temporary deposit. All is in a clear record (Qur'ān 11:6).

In another verse, Allāh Most High says:

﴿وَلَا تَقْتُلُوْا أَوْلَادَكُمْ خَشْيَةَ إِمْلَاقٍ، نَّحْنُ نَرْزُقُهُمْ وَإِيَّاكُمْ، إِنَّ قَتْلَهُمْ كَانَ خِطْئًا كَبِيْرًا﴾

> And kill not your children for fear of want. We shall provide sustenance for them as well as for you. Verily the killing of them is a great sin (Qur'ān 17:31).

Sayyiduna ʿUmar ibn al-Khaṭṭāb ﷺ says, "I heard the Messenger of Allāh ﷺ say:

لو أنكم كنتم توكَّلون على الله حقَّ توكُّله لرُزِقْتم كما يُرزق الطيرُ تغْدو خِماصًا وتروح بطانًا

> If you were to trust Allāh as he ought to be trusted, you would be given sustenance as birds are given it. They go out hungry in the morning and return full in the evening (*Tirmidhī* 2344, *Ibn Māja* 4164).

Thus, contemporary scholars such as Muftī Muḥammad Shafīʿ ʿUthmānī, Muftī Taqi Usmani, and many others mention that practicing contraception due to a fear of poverty is in direct conflict with the established principles of the Sharīʿa. Hence, it would not be permissible to carry out any form of contraception due to a fear of poverty (*Ḍabt-i Wilādat*).

Contraception out of Shame of Conceiving a Girl

Similarly, contraception will be unlawful (*ḥarām*) if practiced for fear and shame of conceiving a girl, as was the custom in the days of ignorance (*jāhiliyya*).

It is well-recorded that the pagan Arabs had a custom of burying newborn girls alive (female infanticide), which the Qur'ān explicitly condemned in Sūrat al-Takwīr. It was regarded as a brutal, barbaric, and inhumane practice. Allāh Most High says:

﴿وَإِذَا الْمَوْءُوْدَةُ سُئِلَتْ، بِأَيِّ ذَنْبٍ قُتِلَتْ﴾

> When the female (infant) that was buried alive is asked for what crime she was killed (Qur'ān 81: 8–9).

And Allāh Most High says:

> When news is brought to one of them, of (the birth of) a female (child), his face darkens, and he is filled with inward grief! With shame does he hide himself from his people, because of the bad news he has had! Shall he retain it on contempt, or bury it in the dust? Ah! What an evil (choice) they decide on? (Qur'ān 16: 58–59).

Thus, practicing any form of contraception for gender selection, whether wanting a boy over a girl or a girl over a boy, is, without doubt, contrary to the teachings of Islam and is thus not permissible.

The Fashion of Having Small Families

Also, contraception will not be permissible for the fashion of keeping small families and conforming to the norm. Desiring to be the average family consisting of a father, mother, daughter, and son, in the hope of fitting in with the common community undermines Islamic principles and relegates it to a status beneath societal customs and norms. Islam encourages procreation, so to practice contraception out of fashion or fad is not permissible.

Population Control

It should also be remembered that the above discussion on reversible contraception and its permissibility is only something that is given as a concession on an individual and personal level. It does not in any way validate the collective and communal endeavor of contraception known as population control.

Striving and lobbying for any type of scheme that calls for the regulation of the human population is clearly contrary to the teachings of the Qur'ān and Sunna. Adopting birth control as a national policy can never be deemed permissible in Islam, for Islam encourages procreation and rejects the fundamental premises of population control.

Muslims should actively participate in teaching the merits of having children and removing any fears of poverty or hardship. Verses of the Qur'ān and the various statements of the Messenger of Allāh ﷺ are quite clear in condemning the systematic control of increases in a population via contraception.

Two Forms of Reversible Contraception

As mentioned earlier, all of the contemporary reversible contraceptive methods have the same ruling as *ʿazl* (coitus interruptus)—that is, permissibility with a slight degree of dislike. Hence, the various methods such as the pill, condom, and injection will fall under the same ruling (but see below for Mālikī prohibition of the pill).

However, the Sharīʿa ruling for two particular methods of contraception is somewhat different. These methods are the "loop" and "emergency contraception."

The Loop

A question with regards to using the loop, as a method of contraception, was posed to one of the renowned contemporary scholars, Shaykh Muftī Taqi Usmani (may Allāh preserve him). The respected Muftī issued a decisive *fatwā* on the issue. Below is the actual text of the question and answer:

Question

The question arises as to whether the use of the loop, which is inserted in the uterus of the woman, is permitted as a means of birth control. The effect of the use of the loop is summarized in the letter of Dr. A.E. Sulayman, an experienced and qualified gynecologist.

In some cases, the sperm and ovum are destroyed prior to fertilization. In other cases, fertilization takes place but the resultant fertilized ovum that takes the form of cellular material is prevented from becoming implanted in the inner wall of the uterus.

In the time of such expulsion of the fertilized ovum, Muftī Jalīl Qāsimī [a scholar referenced by the questioner] has expressed the view that the use of the loop in such circumstances is permissible although not encouraged, such view being based on the analogy of *ʿazl*. A general medical practitioner has raised an objection to the effect that the cellular material that is so expelled contains life but then, in answer, the sperm and the unfertilized ovum also contains life. Your considered *fatwā* on the matter would be greatly appreciated as soon as possible.

Answer

It appears from your question as well as the enclosed explanation given by the expert that the use of the loop may bring either of the two results: (1) it may prevent fertilization by destroying sperm and the ovum prior to their interaction; or (2) if the fertilization takes place, the fertilized ovum is expelled from the uterus by the loop. This expulsion takes place within one or two weeks after the fertilization.

In the first case where the loop acts as a preventive measure against fertilization, it is similar to any other contraceptive and the rules regarding *ʿazl* (coitus interruptus) may be applied to the loop also, i.e., its use is permissible in the Sharīʿa in cases of individual needs, such as the sickness or the weakness of the woman where pregnancy may endanger her health.

In the second case, however, the rules of *ʿazl* cannot be applied, because in that case it is not merely a preventive measure, but it expels the fertilized ovum from the uterus after conception. Therefore, it acts as a device to effect an abortion. Hence, the rules of abortion shall apply.

According to the Islamic rules, an abortion is totally prohibited if it is effected after the completion of 120 days after conception, when the fetus has developed into a human being. But at an earlier stage, an abortion may be permissible for medical reasons or other genuine need.

As the loop expels the fertilized ovum within two weeks, its use cannot be held as totally prohibited. However, being a device of abortion, its use is not advisable and it should be restricted to cases of real medical needs only" (*Contemporary Fatawa* 136–137).

In light of the above *fatwā,* it becomes clear that if a reversible contraceptive device acts after the sperm has fertilized the egg and the device prevents a fertilized egg from implanting itself into the womb, then the ruling on employing such a contraceptive device will be different.

The ruling on such contraceptive devices would be similar to that of carrying out an abortion at an earlier stage, which is impermissible unless there is a genuine and valid reason. Hence, one should abstain from employing such methods of contraception without a genuine medical need.

Emergency Contraception (The Morning-After Pill)

The morning-after pill is estimated to prevent about 85% of pregnancies. It is thought to work by: (a) stopping the ovaries from releasing an egg; (b) preventing sperm from fertilizing any egg that may already have been released; or, importantly, (c) stopping a fertilized egg from attaching itself onto the lining of the womb. Experts state,

> Popularly dubbed the morning-after pill, the drug Levonelle can actually be taken up to 72 hours after intercourse. The 1861 Offences against the Person Act prohibits the supply of any "poison or other noxious thing" with intent to cause miscarriage. SPUC's argument is based on the fact that the drug stops an embryo from implanting in the lining of the womb. The organization successfully applied last year for leave to bring a judicial review of the government's decision to reclassify the drug as suitable for over-the-counter sale. The court will be asked to consider "what is the precise moment at which a woman becomes pregnant." Is it when the egg is fertilized, or when the resulting embryo is implanted in the womb? If it is the former, then the court could rule that emergency contraception causes a miscarriage and is illegal (see the official brochure of Schering Health Care Limited, manufacturer of Levonelle pills).

In light of the above, it can be said that the morning-after pill will have the same ruling as the loop, for it may work in stopping a fertilized egg from attaching itself onto the womb lining. Therefore, the rules of an early abortion would apply in this case also; hence, it should only be used in extreme medical conditions.

In conclusion, the ruling on employing the "loop" or the "morning-after pill" (or any other method that may act after the egg has been fertilized) is somewhat different from the general ruling of reversible contraception. Reversible contraception is generally permitted with a slight degree of dislike, while employing any method that may prevent a fertilized egg from implanting itself into the womb will not be allowed except in certain medical and health situations, examples of which are given in the coming section on abortion (see page 62).

The Mālikī Position on the Pill and Other Medicinal Methods

Coitus interruptus and other contemporary non-hormonal methods of contraception are to be included in the general permissibility of reversible contraception and hence allowed in the Mālikī school. However, the use of any medicine to prevent pregnancy is not allowed according to the traditional opinion in the school, even though some recent Mālikī scholars like Shaykh ʿAbd al-Raḥmān al-Ghiryānī permitted it. The great Mālikī jurist Muḥammad ʿIllīsh, in his compilation of *fatwās* entitled *Fatḥ al-ʿAliyyi 'l-Mālik,* says, "It is not permissible to use medicine to prevent pregnancy . . . Once the semen has entered the womb, it is prohibited to take any measure to remove it" (*Fatḥ al-ʿAliyy al-Mālik fi 'l-Fatwā ʿalā Madhhab al-Imām Mālik* 1: 399). Therefore, since the pill and injection are forms of medication, these methods would be impermissible in the Mālikī school.

Birth Control Patches

A relatively new form of contraception has emerged known as the "Birth Control Patch." Since its introduction in 2001, the contraceptive patch has become an alternative to the pill. The patch is a hormonal method of contraception that can be obtained by prescription. The birth control patch is a 1¾-inch square, thin, beige-colored patch that looks like a square band-aid. It is applied directly to the skin of the buttocks, abdomen, upper torso, or upper outer arm, and releases hormones through the skin into the bloodstream to prevent pregnancy. The patch is replaced weekly on the same day of the week for three consecutive weeks. During the fourth week, no patch is applied to allow the menstrual period to occur. The patch can be safely worn when showering, bathing, exercising, or swimming. However, the patch should not be moved or removed until the week is up once it is applied to the skin, as doing so may cause the patch to become loose.

From an Islamic viewpoint, if birth control is being practiced for a "genuine" medical need and no other alternative method of contraception is available or effective (which is rare), or the other alternatives are considered medically harmful, then a birth control patch will be considered a form of "medical treatment," and hence would take the ruling of other patches or bandages: when there is harm or hardship in removing them, one may simply wipe over them with a wetted hand such that one wipes over most of the area. If, however, there is no such medical need for practicing birth control, or other alternative contraceptive methods are available, effective, and not harmful, one will have to remove the patch and wash the relevant area for the ritual bath (*ghusl*). As such, it will not be permitted to resort to the patch for contraception in this case.

Selling Contraceptives

As for selling the various types of contraceptives, one should keep in mind the juridical principle "Everything that it is possible to use in a permitted manner is lawful to sell" (*Radd al-Muḥtār* 6:391).

Hence, it would be permitted (*ḥalāl*) to sell the various types of contraceptives including the loop and the morning-after pill, as they have legally permissible uses. The morning-after pill (as explained earlier) can be used in cases of medical need; therefore, it would be permitted to sell it. It is analogous to selling a knife: one may use it to cut a fruit, but could use it to stab someone else.

Thereafter, if it is not used lawfully, the seller will not share the sin or blame, because that unlawful action was purely through the deliberate and willful action of the purchaser and not due to the sale itself. One does not even need to ask or investigate why it is being used and the assumption of lawful use is permissible on the part of the seller. However, if, in a particular case, the seller is certain of it being used unlawfully, it would be best to avoid selling it to that particular person.

Disadvantages and Harms of Contraception

At this point, I would like to highlight that, irrespective of the Islamic rulings, birth control in general and the various methods of contraception are associated with many disadvantages and side effects:

1. Contradicting the Sharīʿa motive of marriage, which, as stated earlier, is procreation.

2. Lack of trust in Allāh Most High (if contraception is carried out for economic reasons).

3. One is unaware of which child may be a source of salvation for one in the Hereafter; that is, the semen wasted could be the child who may intercede for one in the Hereafter.

4. After being content and happy with a certain number of children, it is possible that one's children—Allāh forbid—are killed or severely injured in a tragic accident or die a natural death, thus leaving one regretting the situation in one's old age.

5. Sterilizing operations are carried out with associated risks (aside from failure) and can be very harmful for both sexes. Male sterilization risks include bleeding and infection, swelling of the scrotum, and the possibility of sperm granulomas (small, inflamed hard nodules at the end of the severed tube). If these do not heal on their own, surgery may be required. Risks from the female sterilization include bleeding and infections and, in the long run, changes in menstrual cycles, pelvic pain, and the possibility of additional operations. There is much ongoing research investigating the potential long-term risks of both forms of sterilization.

6. One of the major side effects of the pill is the increased risk of thrombosis. Thrombosis is a condition in which the blood changes from a liquid to a solid state within the blood vessel and produces a blood clot or thrombus, which can be detrimental to one's health and life.

7. Prolonged use of the pill increases the risk of certain cancers. Doctors also advise using smaller dose pills.

8. Headaches and fatigue are reported more frequently in people taking a contraceptive pill.

9. The pill does not always work to control the regularity of the menstrual cycle and its use can lead to spotting or irregular bleeding.

10. Some women experience nausea and tiredness. (It would be worthwhile to note here, however, that the side effects of modern day birth control pills are relatively low. Many experts believe that pills used today have much lower dosage than before and are so low in their hormone concentrations that they do not lead to the side effects once commonly associated with the pill. Although particular side effects

have been reduced they can still appear in some women. Some women may experience irregular periods, nausea, headaches, or weight change when taking the oral contraceptive pill, and each pill may affect each woman differently. It would therefore be best to seek the advice of an expert before taking the pill.)

11. Bleeding is the primary side effect linked to the use of an IUD (intra-uterine devices). Women's monthly periods can become slightly heavier and last for longer durations. This can be very troublesome for women, as well as affect her worship and restrict sexual activity.

These are just a few of the harms in practicing contraception; hence, one should abstain from practicing it unless one is in genuine need.

Abortion

Abortion is the termination of a pregnancy via the expulsion of the fetus from the womb through the consumption of certain medications or emptying the womb by suctioning out its contents.

An abortion may be spontaneous or induced. A spontaneous abortion is one that occurs naturally as a result of certain pathological conditions, which are often beyond the control of the pregnant woman and her physician, or due to a physical injury. It is commonly termed a "miscarriage." An induced abortion is the deliberate interruption of pregnancy by artificially inducing the loss of the fetus. Our discussion here will be regarding this type of abortion, for a spontaneous abortion has no connection with Islamic law, since one is not responsible for what is beyond one's control. The Messenger of Allāh ﷺ said, "My Umma has been excused of actions committed by mistake, out of forgetfulness, or by coercion" (*Ṭabarānī*).

Before understanding the Islamic ruling with regard to aborting a pregnancy, it is imperative that we understand a very important Islamic concept.

Life is Sacred

It is a well-established principle of Islam that Allāh Almighty has honored human beings. Allāh Most High says in the Qur'ān:

﴿وَلَقَدْ كَرَّمْنَا بَنِيْ آدَمَ وَحَمَلْنَاهُمْ فِي الْبَرِّ﴾

And verily we have honored the children of Ādam (Qur'ān 17:70).

Thus, it is unlawful (*ḥarām*) to transgress in any way against human life, for it is sacred. Killing a human is considered one of the greatest of sins in the sight of Allāh Most High. He says:

﴿مَنْ قَتَلَ نَفْسًا بِغَيْرِ نَفْسٍ أَوْ فَسَادٍ فِي الْأَرْضِ فَكَأَنَّمَا قَتَلَ النَّاسَ جَمِيْعًا، وَمَنْ أَحْيَاهَا فَكَأَنَّمَا أَحْيَا النَّاسَ جَمِيْعًا﴾

If anyone kills a person—unless it be for murder or for spreading mischief in the land—it is as if he has slain the whole of mankind, and if anyone saves a life, it is as if he has saved the life of the whole of mankind (Qur'ān 5:32).

The jurists (*fuqahā'*) state that in the case of extreme hunger, when there is no alternative available, unlawful things such as pork and alcohol become permissible to consume. However, even in such a situation, consuming or deriving benefit from a human body (cannibalism) remains unlawful. Human beings have been given the highest status of being the noblest of all creatures; hence, the sanctity of human life is beyond that of any other created thing.

It is stated in one of the renowned classical works of Ḥanafī *fiqh, Al-Fatāwā al-Hindiyya,* "If a person fears death by starvation and someone says to him, 'Cut off my hand and eat it,' or says, 'Cut a part of me off and eat it,' it would be unlawful for him to do so. Similarly, it is impermissible for such a person to cut off part of his own body and consume it" (*Al-Fatāwā al-Hindiyya* 5:310).

Imām Ibn ʿĀbidīn (may Allāh have mercy on him) explains, "[...]

because the flesh of a human remains unlawful even in forceful and compelling situations" (*Radd al-Muḥtār* 5:215).

The jurists have also stated that if one is forced into killing another human being, it is still impermissible to do so, even if one's own life was in danger (*Badā'iʿ al-Ṣanā'iʿ* 7:177, *Al-Mughnī* 9:331).

Human life is sacred, whether that life is extra- or intra-uterine, as both are equal and sanctified according to the Sharīʿa. It does not matter where that life exists, for its location neither adds to nor detracts from its sanctity. The life of a baby within its mother's womb is as sacred as the life of a mother according to the Sharīʿa. Thus, it will be necessary to retain its sanctity.

Moreover, the human body is also as sacred as human life. A human body is sacred even after a person dies. The Messenger of Allāh ﷺ said,

كسْرُ عَظم الميِّت ككَسْره حيٍّ

> Breaking the bone of a dead person is similar [in sin] to breaking the bone of a living person (*Abū Dāwūd* 3199, *Aḥmad*).

The great Ḥanafī jurist and ḥadīth expert, Imām Abū Jaʿfar al-Ṭaḥāwī (may Allāh have mercy on him) writes in the explanation of this ḥadīth, "This ḥadīth demonstrates that the bone of a dead person has the same sanctity and honor as the bone of a living person" (*Mushkil al-Āthār*).

In conclusion, the human body, unborn, alive, or dead, has great significance. It is honored and sacred, and because of the sanctity attached to it, it is unlawful to terminate it, tamper with it, cut parts of it off, or dishonor it in any way.

The Islamic Ruling on Abortion

According to the Sharīʿa, abortion can be divided into two types: (1) abortion after the soul (*rūḥ*) has entered the fetus; and (2) abortion prior to the entry of the soul into the fetus.

When Does the Soul Enter the Fetus?

It is imperative to know that according to the Sharīʿa, the soul enters the fetus at 120 days (four months) from the date of conception.

The jurists have based this duration upon a Qur'ānic verse and a statement of the beloved Messenger of Allāh ﷺ. In the verse, Allāh Almighty mentions the stages of embryonic development in the womb of the mother:

﴿وَلَقَدْ خَلَقْنَا الْإِنْسَانَ مِنْ سُلَالَةٍ مِّنْ طِينٍ، ثُمَّ جَعَلْنَاهُ نُطْفَةً فِيْ قَرَارٍ مَّكِيْنٍ، ثُمَّ خَلَقْنَا النُّطْفَةَ عَلَقَةً فَخَلَقْنَا الْعَلَقَةَ مُضْغَةً فَخَلَقْنَا الْمُضْغَةَ عِظَامًا فَكَسَوْنَا الْعِظَامَ لَحْمًا ثُمَّ أَنْشَأْنَاهُ خَلْقًا آخَرَ، فَتَبَارَكَ اللّٰهُ أَحْسَنُ الْخَالِقِيْنَ﴾

> And verily We did create man from a quintessence (of clay). Then We placed him (as a drop of sperm) in a place of rest, firmly fixed. Then We made the sperm into a clot of congealed blood. Then of that clot We made a (fetus) lump. Then We made out of that lump bones and clothed the bones with flesh. Then We developed out of it another creature (by breathing life into it). So blessed be Allāh, the most marvelous Creator (Qur'ān 23:12–14).

In a ḥadīth recorded by the two most reliable authorities, Imām Bukhārī and Imām Muslim (may Allāh have mercy on them both), the Messenger of Allāh ﷺ discussed in detail the periods elapsing between the embryonic stages mentioned in the Qur'ān.

Sayyiduna ʿAbdullāh ibn Masʿūd رضي الله عنه narrates that the Messenger of Allāh ﷺ said,

إنَّ أحدكم يُجمَع خَلْقُه في بطن أمه أربعين يومًا، ثم يكون علقةً مثل ذلك، ثم يكون مُضغةً مثل ذلك، ثم يَبعث الله ملكًا فيُؤمر بأربع كلمات، ويقال له: اكتُبْ عملَه، ورزقَه، وأجلَه، و شقيٌّ أو سعيدٌ، ثم يُنفخ فيه الروح

> Each one of you forms in the womb of his mother for forty days, and then he becomes a clot of thick blood for a similar period, and then a piece of flesh for a similar period. Then Allāh sends an angel who is ordered to

> write four things. He is ordered to write down his deeds, his livelihood, his [date of] death, and whether he will be blessed or wretched [in religion]. Then the soul is breathed into him (*Bukhārī* 3036).

Based on this Qur'ānic verse and ḥadīth, the jurists have concluded that the soul (*rūḥ*) enters the fetus at around four months of gestation.

Imām Ibn ʿĀbidīn (may Allāh have mercy on him) states, "The soul enters the fetus at 120 days (four months), as established by the ḥadīth" (*Radd al-Muḥtār* 1:202).

Thus, when the age of the unborn child reaches 120 days (four months), it no longer remains a lifeless object; rather, it is a living human being. At this point, all organ differentiation is almost completed and the child acquires the shape of a human body.

Ruling on Abortion after 120 Days (Four Months)

When the pregnancy reaches 120 days, an abortion becomes totally forbidden (*ḥarām*) and is tantamount to murder, for it is the taking out of an innocent life and killing the baby in the mother's womb. This is the ruling upon which all the Islamic jurists, past and present, have agreed, unanimously condemning such a ghastly act.

Imām Ibn Taymiya (may Allāh have mercy on him) states in his *Fatāwā,* "Aborting a fetus has been declared unlawful (*ḥarām*) with the consensus of all the Muslim scholars. It is similar to burying an infant alive as referred to by Allāh Most High in the verse of the Qur'ān, 'And when the female infant that was buried alive is asked for what crime she was killed'" (*Majmūʿ al-Fatāwā* 4:217).

Female infanticide was prevalent during the days of ignorance (*jāhiliyya*). The Messenger of Allāh ﷺ commanded that this custom be stopped immediately, and Islam regarded this barbaric act not only un-Islamic but against the very nature of humanity. Thus, Allāh Most High revealed the following verse:

﴿وَإِذَا الْمَوْءُودَةُ سُئِلَتْ، بِأَيِّ ذَنْبٍ قُتِلَتْ﴾

> When the female infant that was buried alive is asked for what crime she was killed (Qur'ān 81:8-9).

Thereafter, female infanticide was completely prohibited.

Muftī Muḥammad Shafiᶜ ᶜUthmānī (may Allāh have mercy on him) comments on this verse of the Qur'ān: "To abort a pregnancy after 120 days will also come under the domain of infanticide, because the soul is entered into the fetus after this period and thereafter it is a living human being" (*Maᶜārif al-Qur'ān* 8:682–683).

As stated previously, all the jurists are unanimous on the impermissibility of aborting a pregnancy after 120 days. Nevertheless, let us take a brief look at what the four major Sunnī schools of Islamic law say in this regard.

The Ḥanafī School

Imām Ibn ᶜĀbidīn (may Allāh have mercy on him), an authority in this school, writes, "If a woman intends to abort the pregnancy, the [Ḥanafī] jurists have stated that if the period of the soul being blown into the fetus (i.e., 120 days) has elapsed, it is not permissible for her to do so" (*Radd al-muḥtār* 6:374).

The Mālikī School

Imām Aḥmad al-Dardīr (may Allāh have mercy on him) states, "When the soul is entered into the fetus [at 120 days], it is unlawful (*ḥarām*) to abort it by consensus" (*Ḥāshiyat al-Dasūqī ᶜala 'l-Sharḥ al-Kabīr* 2:237).

The Shāfiᶜī School

Imām Shihāb al-Dīn al-Ramalī (may Allāh have mercy on him) states, "As for [terminating the pregnancy] after the soul being entered into the fetus is concerned, there is no doubt in its prohibition (*taḥrīm*)" (*Nihāyat al-Muḥtāj ilā Sharḥ al-Minhāj* 8:416).

The Ḥanbalī School

All the Ḥanbalī jurists agree that it is unlawful (*ḥarām*) to abort the pregnancy after the elapsing of four months from conception, as we have seen in the text of Imām Ibn Taymiya quoted above (see also *Al-Inṣāf* 1:386 and *Kashshāf al-Qināʿ* 1:204).

The Situation of Necessity

As stated above, abortion after the expiry of four months is totally unlawful (*ḥarām*) and is held as tantamount to murder. However, the question remains as to whether it is permitted to carry out an abortion (after this stage) in the situation where the mother's life is in serious danger.

Contemporary scholars have differed as to the permissibility of an abortion in such a case. Scholars such as Shaykh Muftī Taqi Usmani of Pakistan, Shaykh Saʿīd Ramaḍān al-Buṭī of Damascus, Muftī Ẓafīr al-Dīn of Dār al-ʿUlūm Deoband, India, and others are of the opinion that even in a situation where the mother's life is in danger, an abortion will not be permitted. This also seems to be the inclination of Ḥakīm al-Umma Mawlānā Ashraf ʿAlī Thānawī (may Allāh have mercy on him) in his *Imdād al-Fatāwā* (4:204).

They state that the Sharīʿa does not allow the termination of one life in order to save the life of another. This principle is derived from works of classical jurists who consider it forbidden to transgress upon a human life even for the purpose of saving one's own life.

It is stated in *Al-Fatāwā al-Hindiyya,* "If one fears death by starvation and someone says to him, 'Cut off my hand and eat it' or says, 'Cut a part of me and eat it,' it is unlawful for him to do so. Similarly, it is impermissible for a desperate person to cut off part of his own body and eat it" (*Al-Fatāwā al-Hindiyya* 5:310).

The jurists have also stated that if one is forced into killing another human, it is not permissible, even if one's own life is in danger (*Badā'iᶜ al-Ṣanā'iᶜ* 7:177, *Al-Mughnī* 9:331).

Moreover, one of the necessary requirements for a situation to be considered a "genuine" situation of need is that the need be immediate, not something expected to play out in the future. As such, it will not be permitted to terminate the life of the unborn child because of medical examinations showing the mother's life to be at risk in the future. Hence, according to this group of scholars, an abortion will remain unlawful after the expiry of 120 days even if the mother's life is in danger (*Taḥdīd al-Nasl* 95–96).

However, some other contemporary scholars have given a dispensation in aborting the pregnancy after 120 days only in the situation where the mother's life is in grave danger. Scholars such as Shaykh Muṣṭafā al-Zarqā', Shaykh Khālid Sayfullāh Raḥmānī and others are of the view that an abortion for fear of the mother dying, will be permitted even after the entry of the soul into the fetus. They have based this ruling on the famous juristic principle, which states, "If one is confronted by two evils, one should choose the lesser of the two" (*Al-Ashbāh wa 'l-Naẓā'ir* 98).

They state that the mother's life may be saved and the fetus aborted, for the mother is established in life, with duties and responsibilities, whereas the unborn child is still in the mother's womb.

As for the statements of the classical scholars with regard to the impermissibility of terminating one life to save another, this is when both lives are equal in existence, which is not the case here. A human who has come into this world has many roles and responsibilities; hence, this human's life is considered complete. On the other hand, the unborn child does not enjoy the same role and responsibility in life and its life cannot be characterized as complete. Therefore, there is a logical distinction between the life of the mother and the life of the unborn child (*Fatāwā Muṣṭafā al-Zarqā'* 286, *Jadīd Fiqhī Mabāḥith* 1:307).

If a pregnant woman is suddenly faced with extreme illness and pains, and medical experts are of the opinion that if she is treated, her unborn child will die, then in such a case, the pregnant mother will have to be treated even if that leads to the loss of her unborn child. The underlying reason is that the mother is being medically treated for her illness and pain, which is the basic right of every human being. The child being lost is merely a natural consequence of treating the mother; hence, this action will not be considered a direct killing of the child. In modern-day ethics, this is called the Principle of Double Effect.

As for when there is a fear of the mother losing her life while giving birth, none of the classical scholars have given explicit permission to terminate the pregnancy; thus, it would not be allowed in general. However, in an extreme case, one may consult a reliable scholar of knowledge and piety and seek his advice.

Ruling on Abortion Before 120 Days (Four Months)

An abortion prior to four months (120 days) is also unlawful (*ḥarām*) in normal situations according to the majority of classical and contemporary scholars, but it will not be classified as murder. This is what we find in the books of the major classical jurists from all four schools of Islamic law.

The Ḥanafī School

Imām Ibn ʿĀbidīn (may Allāh have mercy on him) states, "[Imām Ḥaskafī's statement 'it is prohibitively disliked to carry out an abortion'] meaning at all stages, prior to the formation of the organs and after it . . . except that she [the mother] will not be guilty of committing the sin of murder [if the abortion takes place before four months]" (*Radd al-Muḥtār* 6:429).

He also states, "I would not say that it is permitted [to abort the fetus before its body parts are formed], because a person in the state of pilgrim sanctity (*muḥrim*) is liable to pay a penalty by merely breaking the egg of the hunted animal. . . . Thus, if by merely breaking the egg one has to pay the penalty, then there can be nothing less than committing a sinful act here [in the case of aborting the fetus] if the fetus was aborted without a valid excuse, except that one will not be committing the sin of murder" (*Radd al-Muḥtār* 6:591).

The Mālikī School

The Mālikī school is clear regarding the impermissibility of an abortion once the semen is retained in the womb.

It is stated in *Al-Sharḥ al-Kabīr* of Imām Dardīr, "It is not permissible to take out the semen that has reached the womb, even before the passing of forty days. And when the soul is entered, it becomes absolutely unlawful" (*Ḥāshiyat al-Dasūqī ʿala 'l-Sharḥ al-Kabīr* 2:237).

Another Mālikī jurist, Imām Ibn Juzay (may Allāh have mercy on him) states, "When the womb retains the semen, it becomes impermissible to meddle with it. The sin will become more severe when the organs of the body are formed, and even more when the soul is actually blown into the fetus, for that is considered to be murder by consensus" (*Al-Qawānīn al-Fiqhiyya* 235).

The Shāfiʿī School

Imām Ibn Ḥajar al-Makkī, the great Shāfiʿī jurist, states,

> The scholars have differed in regards to the ruling of causing the pregnancy to be aborted prior to when the soul being entered into the fetus, which is 120 days. Ibn al-ʿImād and others are of the view that it will be unlawful (*ḥarām*). This should not be objectionable due to the permissibility of practicing coitus interruptus (*ʿazl*), because the difference between the two is apparent, in that the semen at the time of ejaculation is a "part of a whole" that is not ready for life in any way, contrary to when it has settled into the womb (*Tuḥfat al-Muḥtāj* 8:241).

Imām Abū Ḥāmid al-Ghazālī (may Allāh have mercy on him) states in his renowned *Iḥyā' ʿUlūm al-Dīn*, after discussing the ruling on contraception (*ʿazl*):

> Contraception (*ʿazl*) is not like abortion or burying the girl alive (*wa'd*),

because abortion is a crime against an existing being, and existence has stages. The first stage of existence is when the semen settles in the womb and mixes with the secretion (fluid) of the woman, and thus it is ready to receive life. Aborting it would be considered a crime. When it becomes a lump of flesh and a clot, the crime becomes graver. And when the soul is blown into the fetus and its creation is complete, the crime becomes even graver. The crime reaches maximum grievousness when it is committed after the fetus is separated from the mother alive (*Iḥyā' ʿUlūm al-Dīn* 2:51).

The Ḥanbalī School

It is stated in the *Al-Inṣāf* of Imām Mardāwī, "It is permissible to drink some medicine to abort the semen (*nuṭfa*), as stated in *Al-Wajīz*. However, Imām Ibn al-Jawzī [the great Ḥanbalī scholar] mentioned in *Aḥkām al-Nisā'* that this is unlawful (*ḥarām*)" (*Al-Inṣāf* 1:386).

The major Ḥanbalī jurist, Imām Ibn Qudāma (may Allāh have mercy on him) writes, "If a pregnant woman drinks medicine that results in aborting the fetus, then she will have to pay blood money (*ghurra*)" (*Al-Mughnī* 7:816).

Conclusion from the Four Schools

In light of the above texts from the various works of classical scholars, it becomes evident that carrying out an abortion even prior to 120 days will be unlawful. Abortion is unlawful (*ḥarām*) at all stages, whether it is before or after 120 days (four months). However, the level of sin varies according to the period in which the abortion is carried out.

One great contemporary scholar, the late Shaykh Muṣṭafā al-Zarqā' of Syria and Jordan (considered a great Ḥanafī jurist, but who held some liberal opinions) also mentions the prohibition of abortion at all stages. He states, "It is possible to say, in light of the various juristic texts, that abortion without a valid excuse is generally unlawful, for it goes against the Prophetic exhortations regarding marriage, procreation, and increasing the Muslim Umma. Also, because it entails terminating a pregnancy after the child's formation, aborting the fetus is a transgression against a being that would become a complete human being" (*Fatāwā Muṣṭafā al-Zarqā'* 285).

He further says that the sin for aborting a fetus prior to forty days will be of a lesser degree, because the organs of the unborn baby have not as yet been created. After forty days, the crime will be graver up until the completion of four months (120 days), after which an abortion will be absolutely unlawful (ibid.).

One of the great twentieth-century scholars of the Indian Subcontinent, Ḥakīm al-Umma Mawlānā Ashraf ʿAlī Thānawī (may Allāh have mercy on him), also takes a similar stance in his brilliant *fatāwā* collection, *Imdād al-Fatāwā.* He states, after quoting the various texts of the classical Ḥanafī jurists: "It becomes clear from the above texts that if professional examination shows the existence of life in the fetus, then to carry out an abortion is absolutely unlawful (*ḥarām*), and it will be considered murder. However, if there is no existence of life, then it will be permissible to terminate the pregnancy for a valid and genuine reason. Without such a reason . . . the transgressor will be sinful, though the ruling of murder will not apply" (*Imdād al-Fatāwā* 4:203).

It is worth remembering here that the reason why abortion prior to the soul entering the body is also not permitted is that the fetus is considered to be part of the mother's body. Just as one's very own life and also all the limbs and organs of the human body are a trust given by the Almighty Creator, so too is the fetus a trust given to the mother by Allāh; hence she will not have a right to abort it.

The only difference here is that the sin of aborting the fetus will be of a lesser degree than aborting it after 120 days. It would not be regarded as murder, rather violating the rights of a human organ entrusted to the mother by Allāh Most High.

Some contemporary scholars have stated that abortion is permissible as long as it is carried out before the forty days of gestation. But this, however, is incorrect, as we have seen from the many evidences presented above. The permission given by some classical jurists to abort the pregnancy, whether before forty days or 120 days, always pertains to the situation where one has a genuine and valid excuse. Without such an excuse, abortion will remain unlawful at all stages, including before forty days.

Abortion in Cases of Need (Prior to 120 Days)

The above ruling with regard to abortion before the passing of four months is in ordinary circumstances. However, Islam is a religion of mercy and does not command anything that is beyond the capability of an individual. Allāh Most High says:

﴿لَا يُكَلِّفُ اللّٰهُ نَفْسًا إِلَّا وُسْعَهَا﴾

Allāh does not burden a soul except that which it can bear (Qur'ān 2:286).

Based on the above verse of the Qur'ān and other such texts of the Qur'ān and Sunna, the jurists have given a dispensation in carrying out an abortion prior to the elapsing of 120 days if there is a genuine and Islamically valid reason.

The famous juristic principle (*qāʿida fiqhiyya*) based on the guidelines of the Qur'ān and Sunna states, "Necessity makes the prohibited lawful" (*Al-Ashbāh wa 'l-Naẓā'ir* 85).

Imām Ḥaskafī (may Allāh have mercy on him) states, "Aborting the pregnancy is permissible for a valid reason, provided the fetus has not yet been formed" (*Radd al-Muḥtār* 6:429).

Imām Ibn ʿĀbidīn (may Allāh have mercy on him) gives an example for a valid excuse by stating, "[Ḥaskafī's statement] 'Abortion will be permissible for a valid reason,' such as when the milk of a pregnant woman ceases and the father of the child is not in a position financially to hire a wet nurse, and there is a fear of the child perishing, they [the jurists] state that it will be permissible to terminate the pregnancy . . .

provided that the period of 120 days has not elapsed. This is permissible because the fetus has not yet developed into a human, and by aborting it we are saving a human life" (ibid.).[4]

Therefore, it will be permitted to have an abortion (prior to 120 days) if there is an Islamically valid excuse. These excuses are of two types: (1) those that affect the mother and (2) those that affect the unborn child.

Those that Affect the Mother

Excuses that effect the mother are (a) the pregnancy constitutes a danger to the mother's physical health; (b) the pregnancy constitutes a danger to the mother's mental health; (c) the pregnancy is caused by rape; and (d) the pregnant woman is severely crippled or suffers from a serious mental illness and is in no position to care for herself, let alone a child, then, if it is possible to place the child for adoption after it is born, an abortion will not be permissible. However, if no such arrangement can be made, it will be permissible to terminate the pregnancy.

Those that Affect the Unborn Child

Many contemporary scholars have stated that if upon medical examination, it is determined that the child will suffer from severe disabilities or will be inflicted by genetic diseases that will cause the child relentless pains, and that the child will be an undue burden for its parents, then it will be permissible to terminate the pregnancy, but again, provided the four months (120 days) have not passed.

4 The same has also been mentioned in *Al-Fatāwā al-Hindiyya* 4:112. It should be noted here that the above text of Imām Ibn ʿĀbidīn in his *Radd al-Muḥtār* refers to the permissibility of abortion in the generally rare case when the milk of the pregnant mother ceases and the father of the child is not in a position financially to hire a wet nurse, and there is a fear of the child perishing. In such a case, it will be permitted to abort the pregnancy, provided the period of 120 days has not elapsed. The child in question is not the one the mother is pregnant with, but a previous baby. The permissibility of abortion has various conditions: (1) the previous child is dependent on the mother's milk; (2) the father cannot hire a wet nurse nor provide alternative nutrition for the child; (3) there is fear that this previous child may perish if the mother's current pregnancy continues; and (4) this is before 120 days. As for when alternative nutrition (even other than breast milk) is available and affordable, then abortion would remain unlawful.

It should be remembered here though that an abortion would not be justified due to minor reasons and excuses. Thus, there should be a certain danger to the pregnant mother or the unborn baby. Mere doubts will not justify the act of aborting the fetus. Moreover, an honest, reliable, and qualified Muslim doctor must advise this. It would be better if a team of specialists, rather than just one person, decides this. One should consult a reliable scholar to confirm the particulars of one's case, for caution should be exercised in all matters related to the lawful and unlawful.

Abortion and Adultery

Pregnancy due to illegitimate sexual intercourse cannot be considered a valid excuse for carrying out an abortion. Islam condemns and rejects illicit sex and everything that may lead to it. Allāh Most High says:

﴿وَلَا تَقْرَبُوا الزِّنَىٰ، إِنَّهُ كَانَ فَاحِشَةً وَسَاءَ سَبِيلًا﴾

> And do not come [even] close to adultery, for it is a shameful [deed] and an evil, opening the road [to other evils] (Qur'ān 17:32).

Islam has also laid down a legal punishment (*ḥadd*) for the one who is guilty of this grievous crime, so that it serves as a deterrent for others.

Nevertheless, it would not be permitted to have an abortion due to unlawful sex, regardless of how many days have elapsed in the pregnancy. An abortion is not the appropriate Islamic answer to illegitimate sex that results in pregnancy; rather, the solution is to eradicate the means that lead to fornication. If the door is left open for aborting pregnancies that occur outside of wedlock, the ensuing consequences could be destructive.

An incident that took place in the time of the Messenger of Allāh ﷺ sheds light on the Islamic viewpoint in this regard. Sayyiduna ʿAbdullāh ibn Burayda ؓ narrates on the authority of his father that

> a woman came to the Messenger of Allāh ﷺ from Ghāmid and said, "O Messenger of Allāh! I have committed adultery, so purify me." He turned her away. On the following day she said, "O Messenger of Allāh! Why do you turn me away? Perhaps, you turn me away as you turned away Māʿiz. By Allāh, I have become pregnant." He ﷺ said, "Well, if you insist upon it, then go until you give birth [to the child]." When she delivered, she came to the Messenger of Allāh ﷺ with the child wrapped in a piece of cloth and said, "Here is the child to whom I have given birth." He ﷺ said, "Go and suckle him until you wean him." When she had weaned him, she came to him with the child, who was holding a piece of bread in his hand and said, "O Prophet of Allāh! Here is the child, as I have weaned him and he eats food." The Messenger of Allāh ﷺ entrusted the child to one of the Muslims and then ordered the punishment. She was put in a ditch up to her chest. He commanded the people to stone her and they did. Khālid ibn al-Walīd came forward with a stone and flung it at her head. Some blood spurted on his face so he cursed her. The Messenger of Allāh ﷺ heard him cursing her, and said, "O Khālid, be gentle. By Him in Whose Hand is my life, she has made such repentance that even if a wrongful tax collector were to make such a repentance, he would be forgiven. Then the Messenger of Allāh ﷺ ordered [for her to be prepared], and he prayed over her and she was buried (*Muslim* 1695).

The above incident clearly illustrates that a pregnancy due to illegitimate sexual intercourse cannot be terminated; rather, it should be carried to its full term. Had abortion been a legitimate option, the Messenger of Allāh ﷺ would have surely advised it to this woman or at least given her the option to do so.

According to the Sharīʿa, a matter of legal punishment is not something that can be taken lightly. A legal punishment (*ḥadd*) should be carried out as soon as possible, but despite this, the Messenger of Allāh ﷺ ordered her to wait until the child was born and had been weaned. He could have advised her to abort the fetus for the legal punishment to be carried out sooner.

This incident also points to the fact that an abortion due to illicit sex will be unlawful at all stages, whether the soul is blown into the fetus or otherwise. The Messenger of Allāh ﷺ did not ask the woman regarding the timing of the pregnancy. Moreover, the unborn baby in the mother's womb is considered honored and sacred, even though it is the direct result of illegitimate sexual intercourse.

It is stated in the famous Ḥanafī *fiqh* text, *Al-Hidāya,* "And the fetus [due to illegitimate sexual intercourse] is [also] honored, as it is not guilty of any wrongdoing, and thus will not be permissible to terminate" (*Al-Hidāya* 2:312).

In other words, the unborn child in the mother's womb is in no way considered a participant in the sin that led to its conception. Hence, it is a severe crime to abort it for the sin of another. It is inhumane and unjust that the unborn child has to pay the price for a sin committed by two people out of wedlock—a sin they desire to conceal from others. One individual cannot bear the burden of another, and every individual must bear his or her own responsibility, a fact outlined by the Qur'ān. Allāh Most High says:

﴿وَلَا تَزِرُ وَازِرَةٌ وِزْرَ أُخْرَىٰ﴾

No bearer of burdens can bear the burden of another (Qur'ān 17:15).

It is clear, then, that an abortion due to illegitimate sexual intercourse cannot be justified. It will remain unlawful after and prior to the soul being entered into the fetus.

Having said that, in some extreme cases an abortion may be permitted. For instance, suppose a young girl below the age of consent is seduced by a mature man and falls pregnant. Would it be permissible in such a case for her to abort the pregnancy and return to her childhood routines or would an abortion still remain unlawful?

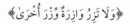

At times, a young girl would prefer suicide rather than give birth to a child conceived out of wedlock. Others may well even leave the religion of Islam altogether if the pregnancy was carried to its full term. All of these are real problems faced by Muslims; hence, a blanket ruling cannot be issued. Each individual case must be taken to a reliable scholar whose knowledge and piety one trusts, and his advice should be sought.

In such extreme cases, some scholars have indeed permitted aborting the fetus. One of the great recent Ḥanafī jurists of the Indian Subcontinent, Muftī Maḥmūd al-Ḥasan Gangōhī (may Allāh have mercy on him), was posed with a question by a doctor regarding a girl who became pregnant due to illegitimate sexual intercourse and was contemplating suicide. He replied with the following answer, recorded in his *fatāwā* collection: "It will be permitted to terminate the pregnancy of the girl who came and confessed that she was pregnant due to unlawful sex, and that she was unmarried, provided that the soul has not yet entered the fetus (i.e., before four months). After the entering of the soul, abortion will not be allowed" (*Fatāwā Maḥmūdiyya* 17:362).

Thus, each individual case will have to be studied separately, and a general ruling cannot be issued. Qualified, knowledgeable and God-fearing scholars will issue a verdict appropriate to each case.

Abortion and Rape

Rape is a sexual crime and is in opposition to adultery and fornication, in the fundamental sense that it is characterized by aggression, force, non-compliance, and violence, whereas unlawful sex is carried out with the consent of both partners. In the unfortunate event of rape, the victim should first resort to immediate medical treatment in order to prevent pregnancy. However, if the pregnancy occurs, then in such a case, many contemporary scholars have permitted terminating the pregnancy provided the stage of the soul being entered into the fetus has not elapsed (120 days).

Many scholars at the Islamic Fiqh Academy of India are of the view that rape is sufficient grounds to justify abortion because classical jurists have permitted abortion for reasons of lesser significance. They state that if a woman is in such a condition of stress and shock that it is impossible for her to face anyone and that she is extremely hurt, it will be permissible for her to abort the pregnancy prior to the passing of 120 days, as this will be considered a genuine and valid reason. In reality, it would be immensely difficult for a woman to be comfortable with a child born out of such a traumatic experience.

The Role of Doctors and Medical Practitioners

Muslim doctors and physicians who are assigned to carry out abortions on their patients must equip themselves with necessary Islamic knowledge concerning abortion and then act in accordance with it. If an abortion is Islamically justified and a Muslim physician determines the presence of an Islamically valid excuse, then there is no bar on him performing the abortion on the patient.

However, in a case where an abortion is not Islamically justified, such as when there is no valid excuse or the pregnancy is over four months old, it is not permitted for a Muslim doctor to carry out an abortion because it would be held as assisting another in a sinful act. One should also avoid forwarding any advice to the patient on how to get an abortion or referring her expressly to another specialist, for that will be considered indirectly leading another to a sin, hence disliked (*makrūh*). Rather, a Muslim physician should attempt to discourage the patient from resorting to an abortion especially if the patient happens to be a Muslim (see *Radd al-Muḥtār* 5: 361).

Conclusion

The various issues discussed in this book can be summarized in the following points:

1. One of the primary objectives of marriage is procreation. Children are a source of mercy granted by Allāh Most High and they are a means of coolness for the parent's eyes. Thus, in general one should abstain from practicing birth control if there is no valid reason to do so.

2. There are two types of contraceptive methods—irreversible and reversible. The irreversible method is carried out by a sterilization operation known as a Vasectomy on the male and a Tubectomy on the female. Reversible contraception refers to the employment of the various temporary methods of contraception, such as coitus interruptus (*ʿazl*), oral contraceptive pills, condoms, intra-uterine devices, injections, and spermicidal jellies.

3. Irreversible (permanent) contraception is totally unlawful (*ḥarām*), although it may be permitted in certain dire and compelling situations.

4. Reversible contraception is considered to be somewhat disliked (*makrūh tanzīhan*) if practiced without a need, and permissible if practiced due to a need. (However, the Mālikī school does not permit the use of medicinal methods of contraception.) This permissibility is only for individual and personal needs, thus to strive for population control can never be permissible under Islamic law or principles.

5. Forms of reversible contraception that prevent pregnancy after the egg has been fertilized, such as the morning-after pill, will not be permitted except in certain limited medical circumstances.

6. Abortion can be divided into two stages—abortion after 120 days and abortion prior to this period.

7. Carrying out an abortion after 120 days (when the soul has entered

the fetus) is totally unlawful by consensus, and is considered to be murder.

8. Abortion prior to 120 days of pregnancy will also be unlawful, although it will not be considered murder. It will become permissible in cases of genuine need and necessity, such as the life and health of the mother being in danger, or if it is feared that the unborn child will be born with severe disabilities.

9. Abortion due to illegitimate sexual intercourse cannot be justified; for the unborn child in the mother's womb is considered to be sacred. However, an abortion due to rape may be permitted, provided that 120 days have not passed after conception.

10. The role of Muslim doctors and medical experts is very important. Hence, they must educate themselves of the Islamic rulings relating to birth control and abortion and act in accordance with them.

Bibliography

Abū Dāwūd, Sulaymān ibn al-Ashʿath. *Kitāb al-Sunan*. Edited by Muḥammad ʿAwwāma. 5 vols. Beirut, Lebanon: Mu'assasat al-Rayyān, Makka, Saudi Arabia: Al-Maktaba al-Makkiyya, and Jeddah, Saudi Arabia: Dār al-Qibla, 1419/1998.

Ali, Abdullāh Yusuf. *The Meaning of the Holy Qur'ān*. Brentwood, USA: Amana Corp., 1996.

al-ʿAsqalānī, Ibn Ḥajar. *Fatḥ al-Bārī Sharḥ Ṣaḥīḥ al-Bukhārī* (a commentary on Bukhārī's *Al-Jāmiʿ al-Ṣaḥīḥ*). Edited by Muḥammad Fu'ād ʿAbd al-Bāqī. 15 vols. Riyadh, Saudi Arabia: Dār al-Salām, 1421/2000.

al-ʿAynī, Badr al-Dīn Maḥmūd ibn Aḥmad. *ʿUmdat al-Qārī Sharḥ Ṣaḥīḥ al-Bukhārī* (a commentary on Bukhārī's *Al-Jāmiʿ al-Ṣaḥīḥ*). 16 vols. Beirut, Lebanon: Dār al-Fikr, 1422/2002.

al-Bahūtī, Manṣūr ibn Yūnus. *Kashshāf al-Qināʿ ʿan Matan al-Iqnāʿ*. Edited by Muḥammad Amīn al-Ḍinnāwī. 5 vols. Beirut, Lebanon: 1417/1997.

al-Bukhārī, Muḥammad ibn Ismāʿīl. *Ṣaḥīḥ al-Bukhārī*. Edited by Muṣṭafā' Dīb al-Bughā. 7 vols. Damascus, Syria and Beirut, Lebanon: Dār Ibn Kathīr and Yamāma, 1414/1993.

al-Būṭī, Muḥammad Saʿīd Ramaḍān. *Mas'ala Taḥdīd al-Nasal Wiqāyatan wa ʿIlājan*. Damascus, Syria: Dār al-Fārābī, 1409/1998 (4th edition).

al-Dardīr, Aḥmad ibn Muḥammad, Khalīl ibn Isḥāq al-Jundī, Muḥammad ʿArafa al-Dasūqī and Muḥammad ibn Aḥmad ʿIllīsh. *Ḥāshiyat al-Dasūqī ʿala 'l-Sharḥ al-kabīr* (Dardīr's commentary on Khalīl's *Mukhtaṣar*, super-commentary by Dasūqī with footnotes from ʿIllīsh Mālikī). 4 vols. Beirut, Lebanon: Dār al-Fikr, 1423/2002.

Gangōhī, Maḥmūd al-Ḥasan. *Fatāwā Maḥmūdiyya* (Urdu). Edited by Muḥammad Fārūq. 17 vols. Karachi, Pakistan: Kutub Khānā Maẓharī, 1406/1986.

al-Ghazālī, Abū Ḥāmid. *Iḥyā' ʿUlūm al-Dīn* (with notes on its ḥadīths by Zayn al-Dīn al-ʿIrāqī). 4 vols. Beirut, Lebanon: ʿĀlam al-Kutub, 1347/1929.

al-Ḥaskafī, Muḥammad ibn ʿAlī, Muḥammad Amīn ibn ʿĀbidīn and Muḥammad ibn ʿAbdillāh al-Tumurtāshī. *Ḥāshiya Radd al-Muḥtār ʿala 'l-Durr al-Mukhtār Sharḥ Tanwīr al-Abṣār* (Ḥaskafī's commentary on Tumurtāshī's *Tanwīr al-Abṣār* printed with the super-commentary of Ibn ʿĀbidīn). 8 vols. Karachi, Pakistan: H.M. Saʿīd Company, 1406/1986.

Ibn ʿĀbidīn, Muḥammad Amīn, *Radd al-Muḥtār ʿala 'l-Durr al-Mukhtār.* Beirut, Lebanon: Dār Iḥyā' al-Turāth al-ʿArabī, 1419/1998.

Ibn al-Humām, Kamāl al-Dīn Muḥammad ibn ʿAbd al-Wāḥid al-Siwāsī. *Sharḥ Fatḥ al-Qadīr ʿala 'l-Hidāya Sharḥ Bidāyat al-Mubtadī* (Ibn al-Humām's commentary of Marghīnānī's *Hidāya* printed with Bābartī's commentary of the *Hidāya* known as *Al-ʿInāya*). 10 vols. Beirut, Lebanon: Dār al-Fikr, second edition.

Ibn Kathīr, Ismāʿīl ibn ʿUmar. *Tafsīr al-Qur'ān al-ʿAẓīm.* 4 vols. Damascus, Syria: Maktaba Dār al-Fayhā', 1418/1998.

Ibn Māja, Muḥammad ibn Yazīd al-Qazwīnī. *Al-Sunan.* Beirut, Lebanon: Dār Iḥyā' al-Turāth al-ʿArabī, 1421/2000.

Ibn Nujaym, Zayn al-Dīn ibn Ibrāhīm. *Al-Ashbāh wa 'l-Naẓā'ir ʿalā Madhhab Abī Ḥanīfa al-Nuʿmān.* Beirut, Lebanon: Dār al-Kutub al-ʿIlmiyya, 1413/1993.

Ibn Qudāma al-Maqdisī, Muwaffaq al-Dīn ʿAbdullāh ibn Aḥmad. *Al-Mughnī.* 11 vols. Beirut, Lebanon: Dār Iḥyā' al-Turāth al-ʿArabī, 1413/1993.

ʿIllīsh, Muḥammad. *Fatḥ al-ʿAliyy al-Mālik fī 'l-Fatwā ʿalā Madhhab al-Imām Mālik.* Beirut, Lebanon: Dār al-Fikr.

Kamali, Muhammad Hashim. *Principles of Islamic jurisprudence.* Cambridge, England: Islamic Texts Society, 1991.

Kanʿān, Muḥammad Aḥmad. *Uṣūl al-Muʿāshara al-Zawjiyya.* Beirut, Lebanon: Dār al-Bashā'ir al-Islāmiyya, 1419/1999.

al-Kāsānī, ʿAlā' al-Dīn Abū Bakr ibn Masʿūd. *Badā'iʿ al-Ṣanā'iʿ fī Tartīb al-Sharā'iʿ.* 7 vols. Quetta, Pakistan: Maktaba Rashīdiyya, 1410/1990.

Mālik ibn Anas. *Al-Muwaṭṭā.* Edited by Bashshār ʿAwwād Maʿrūf. 2 vols. Beirut, Lebanon: Dār al-Gharb al-Islāmī, 1417/1997.

al-Mardāwī, ʿAlā' al-Dīn ʿAlī ibn Sulaymān. *Al-Inṣāf fī Maʿrifat al-Rājiḥ min al-Khilāf.* Edited by Muḥammad Ḥāmid al-Faqqī. 12 vols. Beirut, Lebanon: Dār Iḥyā' al-Turāth al-ʿArabī and Mu'assasat al-Tārīkh al-ʿArabī, second edition.

al-Mawṣilī, ʿAbdullāh ibn Maḥmūd ibn Mawdūd. *Al-Ikhtiyār li Taʿlīl al-Mukhtār.* Edited by Adnān Darwīsh. 3 vols. Beirut, Lebanon: Dār al-Arqam, 1420/1999.

Muslim ibn al-Ḥajjāj, and Yaḥyā ibn Sharaf al-Nawawī. *Ṣaḥīḥ Muslim* with Nawawī's commentary. Edited by Muḥammad Fu'ād ʿAbd al-Bāqī. Beirut, Lebanon: Dār Ibn Ḥazm, 1423/2002.

al-Nawawī, Yaḥyā ibn Sharaf. *Al-Majmūʿ Sharḥ al-Muhadhdhab* (Shīrāzī's *Al-Muhadhdhab* printed with Nawawī's interlinear commentary, which is completed by Subkī's supplement *Takmilat al-Majmūʿ*). Edited by Muḥammad Najīb al-Mutīʿī. 23 vols. Beirut, Lebanon: Dār Iḥyā' al-Turāth al-ʿArabī, 1422/2001.

———. *Al-Minhāj bi Sharḥ Ṣaḥīḥ Muslim ibn al-Ḥajjāj* (commentary by Nawawī on Muslim's *Ṣaḥīḥ*). Beirut, Lebanon: Dār Ibn Ḥazm, 1423/2002.

Mawlānā Niẓām and committee of scholars from the Indian Subcontinent under the supervision of the Moghul Emperor Aurengzeb. *Al-Fatāwā al-Hindiyya* (*ʿĀlamghīriyya*), printed with *Fatāwā Qāḍīkhān* and *Fatāwā Bazzāziyya.* 6 vols. Reprint. Quetta, Pakistan: Maktaba Majīdiyya, 1403/1983.

al-Qārī, ʿAlī ibn Sulṭān. *Mirqāt al-Mafātīḥ Sharḥ Mishkāt al-Maṣābīḥ.* 11 vols. Multan, Pakistan: Maktaba Imdādiyya, 1390/1970.

al-Qāsimī, Mujāhid al-Islām and committee of contemporary scholars from India. *Jadīd Fiqhī Mabāḥith* (Urdu). 17 vols. Karachi, Pakistan: Idārat al-Qur'ān wa 'l-ʿUlūm al-Islāmiyya, 1415/1994.

al-Ramalī, Aḥmad ibn Ḥamza ibn Shihāb al-Dīn and Yaḥyā ibn Sharaf al-Nawawī. *Nihāyat al-Muḥtāj ilā Sharḥ al-Minhāj* (printed with super-commentaries of Shabrāmblusī and Maghribī Rashīdī, in Shāfiʿī *fiqh*). 8 vols. Beirut, Lebanon: Dār Iḥyā' al-Turāth al-ʿArabī, 1412/1992.

Shaykh, Allie Harun. *Islamic Principles on Family Planning.* Karachi, Pakistan: Dār al-Ishāʿat, 1999.

al-Ṭabarānī, Sulaymān ibn Aḥmad. *Al-Muʿjam al-Ṣaghīr.* Edited by ʿAbd al-Raḥmān Muḥammad ʿUthmān. 2 vols. in 1. Madīna, Saudi Arabia: Al-Maktaba al-Salafiyya, 1388/1968.

Thānawī, Ashraf ʿAlī. *Imdād al-Fatāwā* (Urdu). Edited by Muḥammad Shafīʿ ʿUthmānī. 6 vols. Karachi, Pakistan: Maktaba Dār al-ʿUlūm.

al-Tirmidhī, Muḥammad ibn ʿĪsā ibn Sawra. *Al-Jāmiʿ al-Ṣaḥīḥ.* Edited with commentary by Aḥmad Muḥammad Shākir. 5 vols. Beirut, Lebanon: Dār Iḥyāʾ al-Turāth al-ʿArabī.

Usmani, Muhammad Taqi. *Contemporary Fatāwā.* Lahore and Karachi, Pakistan: Idāra Islāmiyyāt, 1999.

ʿUthmānī, Muḥammad Shafīʿ and Muhammad Taqi Usmani. *Ḍabt-i Wilādat kī ʿAqlī wa Sharʿī Heythiyyat* (Urdu). Karachi, Pakistan: Dār al-Ishāʿat, 1983.

———ʿUthmānī, Muḥammad Shafīʿ. *Maʿārif al-Qurʾān* (Commentary of the Qurʾān in Urdu). 8 vols. Karachi, Pakistan: Idārat al-Maʿārif, 1416/1996.

ʿUthmānī, Shabbīr Aḥmad. *Tafsīr ʿUthmānī* (commentary of the Qurʾān with translation of the Qurʾān by Muftī Maḥmūd al-Ḥasan). Azaadville, South Africa: Madrasa Arabiyya Islamiyya, 1420/1999.

al-Zarqāʾ, Muṣṭafā Aḥmad. *Fatāwā Muṣṭafā al-Zarqāʾ.* Edited by Majd Aḥmad al-Makkī. Damascus, Syria and Beirut, Lebanon: Dār al-Qalam, 1420/1999.

Index

B

C

D

E

F

G

H

I

About the Author

Muftī Muhammad ibn Adam al-Kawthari is a traditionally trained scholar who studied in different parts of the world. Born in Leicester, UK and raised under the guidance of his illustrious father, Mawlānā Ādam, he started learning about Islam from a very young age and memorized the Qur'ān at the age of nine. He initially studied the Arabic Language and various other traditional Islamic Sciences at Darul Uloom, Bury, UK, under many Shaykhs notably, Shaykh Muhammad Yusuf Motala and received *ijāzas* in various books including the six major books of ḥadīth.

After graduating from the Darul Uloom, he traveled to Karachi, Pakistan, where he studied under one of the greatest living scholars, Justice (Rtd.) Muftī Muhammad Taqi Usmani and others. Later, he traveled to Damascus, Syria, where he increased in experience and knowledge by studying under the great *ʿulamāʾ* there and received authorization (*ijāza*) from Shaykh ʿAbd al-Razzāq al-Ḥalabī, Shaykh Dr. ʿAbd al-Laṭīf Farfūr al-Ḥasanī and others.

His other works include: *The Issue of Shares* and *Simplified Rules of Zakat.* He has also published Shaykh Muḥammad Zakariyya Kāndhlawī's *Wujūb iʿfāʾ al-liḥya* (*The obligation of growing a beard*) and Shaykh Khalīl Aḥmad Sahāranpūrī's *Mabāḥith fī ʿaqāʾid Ahl al-Sunna* (*Discussions in the beliefs of the People of the Sunna*), both with critical analysis and footnotes in Arabic. He is also widely known for his detailed and well-researched *fiqh* related articles on Qibla (www.qibla.com). He presently resides in Leicester, UK, where he is a teacher of various traditional Islamic sciences at Jamiah Uloom al-Qur'ān, and helps people with their queries and problems at the Institute of Islamic Jurisprudence (Darul Iftaa, www.daruliftaa.com).

Also from
WHITE THREAD PRESS

Prayers for Forgiveness

The Path to Perfection

Saviours of Islamic Spirit

Sufism & Good Character

The Differences of the Imāms

Provisions for the Seekers

Ghazālī's The Beginning of Guidance

Reflections of Pearls

Fiqh al-Imam: Key Proofs in Hanafi Fiqh

The Islamic Laws of Animal Slaughter

Absolute Essentials of Islam

Ṣalāt & Salām: A Manual of Blessings on Allāh's Beloved

Imām Abū Ḥanīfa's Al-Fiqh al-Akbar Explained

Ascent to Felicity (Marāqī 'l-Saʿādāt)

The Book of Wisdoms (Ikmāl al-Shiyam)

The Shāfiʿī Manual of Purity, Prayer & Fasting

White Thread
PRESS

www.whitethreadpress.com